# Preparing Your Church for Revival

## T. M. Moore

With a foreword and annotated bibliography by
Dr. John H. Armstrong

Christian Focus
Reformation & Revival Ministries

Christian Focus Publications

Christian Focus Publications publishes biblically-accurate books for adults and children. The books in the adult range are published in three imprints.
*Christian Heritage* contains classic writings from the past.
*Christian Focus* contains popular works including biographies, commentaries, doctrine, and Christian living.
*Mentor* focuses on books written at a level suitable for Bible College and seminary students, pastors, and others; the imprint includes commentaries, doctrinal studies, examination of current issues, and church history.

For a free catalogue of all our titles, please write to
Christian Focus Publications,
Geanies House, Fearn,
Ross-shire, IV20 1TW, Great Britain

For details of our titles visit us on our web site
http://www.christianfocus.com

ISBN 1 85792 698 6

Published in 2001 by
Christian Focus Publications
Geanies House, Fearn, Ross-shire,
IV20 1TW, Great Britain
and
Reformation & Revival Ministries, Inc.
P.O. Box 88216
Carol Stream, Illinois 60188 USA

Cover design by Alister MacInnes

# Contents

A Slow Reviving
Shaver's Fork, Cheat River
Elkins, West Virginia

The freshening rains fell softly through the night,
fell down upon the trees and trickled down
gnarled grooves of branch and bark to soak the ground
and fill the thirsty conduits out of sight
beneath the forest floor, where they were borne
down hillsides toward the rocky river bed
which lay exposed and parched, like bones long dead,
the day before; smooth stones and boulders worn
and carried down from the surrounding mountain heights
through untold years of nature's sculpting, lay
unwashed just yesterday, but as the day
plods on, with each arrival of the night's
refreshing rains, are gradually baptized in
the river's slow reviving once again.

# Foreword

In 1970 I saw and experienced the dramatic reality of revival. It was only a brief shower on my college campus. But it truly was a divine moment, as one later called it. The actual showers fell for only a few days. But the results have endured for thirty plus years. Lives were touched deeply, professing Christians were truly born from above, missionaries were called and later sent, ministers were raised up by God's grace and began to prepare for future service, indeed entire lives and personal agendas were altered radically. Twenty-five years later I heard scores of my classmates, at a reunion, recall these hours. They testified about how this moment, these showers, changed them forever. What God sometimes does in a moment is indeed striking. Such a moment in time can bear eternal fruit. Make no mistake about it.

But revivals do not last. That is the nature of the case. In fact, we could not live forever in the rain. We need sunshine and cool breezes too. Even fall and winter have a proper place in the cycle of our personal life and in the seasons of our churches as well. Revivals do come, like rain clouds, with needed moisture for dry lands and cold hearts. When they do come they leave behind 'a blessing.' This blessing is so needed in the church of our time. No one who loves the cause of Zion can seriously doubt this analysis. It is needed in almost every local church I know in North America and Europe. It is needed in our fellowships, our schools and our Christian societies.

But there is so much confusion about revival in our time.

A perusal of the titles and numerous books on the subject is enough to confuse the average reader to the point of despair. I think the enemy must delight in this confusion. I feel sure he is pleased that God's people either claim too much when they talk about revival or they seek far too little. So long as the church remains in the dark about this vital subject multitudes will neither pray for God to 'open the heavens' nor prepare the ground of their hearts for the showers we so desperately need. And as long as wrong-headed claims about revival are left unchallenged, the good work of true revival, so needed, will be shunned and even rejected by more sensitive believers who fear more excess and silliness.

What are we to do? First, we must understand what revival is. Definition, in this case, is the first way to win the struggle. He who defines the direction and focus will surely lead the way. In *Preparing Your Church for Revival*, my friend and associate, T. M. Moore, has written a little book that not only defines revival properly but practically helps pastors and church leaders *prepare* their flocks for the work that many of us believe must come.

Brian Edwards, in an extremely important work aptly titled, *Can We Pray for Revival?* (Darlington, England: Evangelical Press, 2001), gets the definition right on the opening page when he says:

Revival is a sovereign work of God's Holy Spirit that produces an unusual awakening of spiritual life among God's people, resulting in an awesome awareness of God, a sincere repentance for sin, a deep longing for God and holiness, and an effective passion to reach the unsaved. It is generally accompanied by a significant number of the lost coming to true faith in Christ.

But we need more than a good definition of revival. T. M. Moore, who heartily agrees with the definition above, also believes we can and must make *preparation* for what the Lord might soon do. We know what God has done in the past. We know that in the midst of judgment and wrath He has sent merciful showers. We know also that we cannot force His hand. We dare not even try. We cannot dictate to the almighty sovereign God what His agenda must be. But His people will ask Him whenever He sends merciful blessings to them. He is still found by those who seek Him and still does perform great acts of mercy on behalf of all who trust and obey Him. The agenda is His; the timing must necessarily belong to the Lord. But the asking and preparing is our human responsibility. Nothing in the Bible contradicts this conclusion. The best and fullest theology supports this balanced theological conclusion.

T. M. Moore understands this. That is what makes this little book so valuable. T.M. is a spiritual guide, a mentor, for leaders and fellow prayer warriors in the church. He is a man of the Word, a man who loves the truth. He is also a man who is practical and helpful through and through. Here the pastor and lay leader has a resource to guide groups into careful preparation for what God might well do in our time.

If revival is a divinely sent fire from heaven, a spiritual blessing that burns off the dross of our lives and restores to us the power, passion and holiness of our first love, then this book may well be a log to put on the pile of our praying and resting in the gracious good will of the God who delights to remember mercy before he sends wrath. Indeed, this little book could well be the catalyst that God uses to begin a great movement of prayer and confession that might result in modern revival. Think of T. M.'s work as high-octane fuel, written by a man who loves the church of Jesus Christ and longs to see her full of his glory once again. I pray his 'fuel' will ignite churches with longing for a true visitation of God in our time.

**John H. Armstrong**

# Introduction

*A voice calling: Prepare the way of the LORD in the wilderness; make a straight highway for our God* (Isaiah 40:3).

It is impossible to read the first eight chapters of the *Book of Acts* and not see that those first Christians were a decidedly different group of people than the folks around them. For that matter, they were decidedly different from most of those today who claim to be their spiritual descendants. They drank daily deep drafts from the fountain of God's truth at the feet of the greatest teachers and evangelists the Church has ever known. They gathered regularly in each other's homes, sharing their meals, worshipping with joy and excitement, encouraging one another in their faith in Jesus Christ, and spending long hours in prayer. Gladly they liquidated their assets and drew down their bank accounts to meet the needs of those who lacked among them. Boldly they resisted the threats of civil government and the dominant religious order to proclaim the faith of Jesus Christ in the streets of Jerusalem. And, when persecution finally broke out with a vengeance, they left everything and took their faith to the surrounding villages and towns, to the nations next door, and to the farthest ends of the earth. They were *indomitable* in their faith; nothing could stop them from celebrating the Lord, serving one another in love, proclaiming the Good News with power, and planting new churches wherever they went. Within a generation they were said to have turned their world upside-down for Jesus Christ.

The difference between them and us is simple. They were a *revived* people, a people filled with and led by the Holy Spirit of God, Who drew them into ever deeper levels of Christian life and witness. They were not only alive, but alive in Christ, and daily renewed in Him such that He became the focus and end of all their activities. They completely defined themselves in terms of their lives in Him, so much so, in fact, that in Antioch, their pagan neighbors, seeking a way to describe these people, referred to them by what seemed most to be on their minds and lips – the Lord Jesus Christ Himself. They called them 'Christians' because, as the people of that pagan city saw it, He was clearly what they were all about. They went about with a new outlook, a new sense of mission and purpose, and in a power that brought forth the new reality of the Kingdom of God which had broken out among them. Their neighbors were amazed by the love they saw among them and stunned by the message they proclaimed; and the Spirit of revival that dwelled within them moved easily through them to draw others into the rapidly-growing community of Christ.

It is not necessary to belabor the sad contrast between those first Christians and the state of God's churches today. Indeed, there is a growing sense within the Christian community that, so unlike these first believers have we become, we are today a people in need of revival.

For many of us perhaps, the word, 'revival,' may not sound very contemporary or upbeat. It conjures up images of Bible-thumping evangelists haranguing sweaty, tired church members with their failure in the line of duty, warning the lost to repent or perish, and soaking up as much of the glory and offerings for themselves as they can. We tend to think of a revival as a week of meetings designed to infuse some new life into the bleached bones of a parched and lifeless congregation, during which a hired-gun evangelist relieves grateful church members of their duty to proclaim the Gospel to their lost neighbors. For many, revival is an old-fashioned word and would appear to be out of sync with the interests and needs of a postmodern culture.

But this is not the Biblical idea of revival; it's not even the predominant way in which revival has been understood during the history of the Church.

A revival is a period of sudden, unusual stirring of God's Spirit among His people. Revival, in other words, is something that *God* does, not something that we sponsor or conduct. God alone can produce revival. Periods of revival come intermittently to the Church, as God is pleased to give them. Solomon Stoddard, who saw many such periods during his glorious ministry in the late-seventeenth and early eighteenth centuries, wrote, 'There are some special seasons wherein God doth in a remarkable Manner revive Religion among his People. God doth not always carry on his Work in the Church in the same Proportion.'[1] During periods of revival all the typical marks of vital Christian life and activity are present. Individuals come to faith in Jesus Christ; churches grow; indications of the love of Christ are present in a wide variety of ways; new enterprises of faith and mission appear; and men and women in unusual numbers respond to the call to serve the Lord in ministry in various ways. The difference is that, *during a revival, all these indications of spiritual vitality are greatly exaggerated and extended.* In particular, evidence of the fruit of the Spirit, and especially the love of Jesus Christ, abounds more and more:

> If a revival is a larger giving to the church of grace already possessed – a heightening of the normal – then it follows that the evidences by which revivals are to be judged are the same as those which form the permanent evidences of real Christianity. Foremost in the New Testament list is the evidence of love to God and men.[2]

When revival is extended to encompass a broad scope of the Church of Christ across a wide geographic swath, sustained for a relatively long period of time, this is called an awakening. Throughout the history of the Church there have been several periods of awakening.

The first three centuries, from Pentecost to the Council of Nicea (325 AD) saw what was undoubtedly the most remarkable season of awakening. During this time, against overwhelming odds, the Christian faith became established throughout the Roman world and beyond, bringing in its train spiritual, moral, social, and cultural renewal such as the Roman world had never known.

A little over a hundred years later a new season of awakening erupted that lasted for nearly 350 years. This revival began among Irish monks and spread from that remote island to Scotland, Wales, and all of Europe. So powerful and dramatic were the effects of this awakening that one author has written of how 'the Irish saved civilization' through their fervent faith in Jesus Christ.[3]

The period of the Protestant Reformation (1517-1648) saw the next great season of awakening and revived faith. The entire Christian world was affected by its energy, including the Roman Catholic Church, which entered into its own season of renewal as a result. The Gospel and the Kingdom of Christ reached to new lands and peoples, through the work of Protestant and Catholic missionaries alike. New applications of the Gospel to the whole of life helped to generate the scientific revolution and to advance the arts and learning. Many scholars trace the rise of democratic and republican forms of civil government to the impulse of the Reformation.

In this country, the First Great Awakening of the 1740s and the Second Great Awakening during the first thirty years of the nineteenth century are perhaps the best-known periods of awakening, followed closely by the revival of 1858-60. The Welsh revival of 1905 is the most recent period during which the Church has seen the Spirit of God moving with the power of an awakening.[4]

During each of these seasons of awakening, the Spirit of God worked in extraordinary measure among His people. Faithful ministers and evangelists proclaimed the Gospel with irresistible power, and millions of people came to saving faith in Jesus Christ or saw their faith in Him renewed and revitalized. Existing churches were suddenly and remarkably awakened, as though baptized with the Spirit all over again; new churches sprang up by the thousands, with multitudes of enthusiastic worshipers; and the knowledge of God and the news of His Kingdom were proclaimed in previously barren regions. New enterprises of faith came into being – schools, missions, cultural endeavors, publication of Bibles and Christian literature, and agencies of social welfare and relief. Moral and social reform followed wherever the Gospel took root. Each period of awakening broadened the beachhead of faith in a sinful world, providing a firmer hold for the Church and a jumping-off place for increased growth and revival.

Far more frequent than these times of awakening, however, are the seasons of revival that have been visited upon local congregations, or congregations within a more limited geographic region.[5] During these periods of revival all the observable signs of spiritual interest are present, not on the same wide scale as in an awakening, or with the same magnitude, but above and beyond what is normally the case. Churches have been remarkably affected by the Spirit of God as He stirs among His people, channeling to and through them renewed energies of grace and power to further the Kingdom purposes of Christ. The pages of Church history are rife with examples of such revivals, even during the darkest years of Gospel light. We have every reason to believe that, as God has revived churches and awakened whole peoples in the past, He will continue to do so throughout the age of the Church until the return of our Lord. Which means that He could do so in our day as well.

So extraordinary are these seasons of revival that they engender a kind of natural skepticism on the part of many who observe them. Indeed, one of the marks of true revival is determined opposition to it, even among those who are recognized as Church leaders. It is therefore essential that Christian leaders be able to identify the marks of true revival and prepare themselves and their churches to participate in such works of the Spirit as He moves according to His good pleasure among His people. Jonathan Edwards warned against being an obstacle in the way of God's reviving work: 'Let us all be warned, *by no means to oppose, or do any thing in the least to clog or hinder the work; but, on the contrary, do our utmost to promote it.*[6] To oppose revival, he believed, was to become 'guilty of the unpardonable sin against the Holy Ghost.'[7]

God wants His people to seek His reviving grace. Complacency is one of the greatest sins a church can abide. Neither hot nor cold, the complacent church runs the risk of being rejected as an effective vessel in the Lord's Kingdom (Rev. 3:16). One of the most frequent supplications of the psalms is for God's reviving and renewing grace (cf. Pss. 69, 80, 85, 119). God is willing to revive His Church. Indeed, He *prefers* her in all her vibrancy, joy, and delight in Him, for then she is truly the delight of the nations ( Ps. 48.1-3). But He calls His people to *seek* His reviving grace and to prepare for it in faith, demonstrating thereby that they fully expect their faithful Covenant God to keep His Word and revive them again.

While revival and awakening appear to be sudden stirrings of God's Spirit, in fact they come gradually, in many unseen ways. The drizzles of God's grace begin to fall in the lives of individuals, drawing them to seek greater downpours of His latter rains and the re-immersion of the stony hearts of His people in the refreshing waters of His grace. Such people become the unseen conduits of God's grace. Having prepared themselves for revival, they urge and equip others to make ready for a new season of the showers of blessing. As the reviving grace of God begins again to fall on His people, these on whom His showers first appeared serve as channels of renewal for whole communities of the people of God.

There are growing indications that God's Spirit may be

starting to stir among His people once again.[8] A ground swell is emerging of longing for revival, praying and preparing for it, teaching and preaching about it, trusting God and calling upon Him to bring it about in our day, to our churches, the nations, and the world. Clearly, the drizzles of grace have begun amid the darkness of our present spiritual night. And revival will surely come, just as it has in the past, but in God's time, not ours. We cannot coax or cajole Him into reviving our churches. We cannot require Him to conform to our programs or agendas. He will accomplish this work, as He has in the past, in His way and time, using the vessels of His choice, and to whatever extent He is pleased to do it.

Yet for our part, believing that God wants His churches to be revived, and understanding that revival, while it is God's work, comes through the agency of chosen human vessels, we must encourage one another, and particularly the shepherds of God's flocks, to devote themselves to preparing their congregations for the stirring of God's Spirit, creating an expectancy, indeed, a *longing* for revival, on the part of the people of God. For it is certain that, as no disciple will rise above his teacher, so no congregation will prepare for or experience revival unless led by its shepherds. Pastors and church leaders, therefore, hold an important key to a renewed stirring of God's Spirit among His people. As was proclaimed in Scotland a century ago concerning the work of pastors in preparing for revival, 'These pastors will embark with such resolute and unflinching determination in the work that they will give him no rest, they will not let him go untill (*sic*) he blesses the church.'[9]

But the people of God as a whole can play an important

role in helping pastors and their churches to take the steps of faith that will show to the sovereign, waiting God that His people eagerly desire a renewed season of His reviving grace. This book comes with the hope that it will provide guidance and encouragement to pastors and church members who, seeking revival for their congregations and the people of God as a whole, are willing to give of themselves to lead their churches in preparing for this mighty work. In the course of our study we will examine, first, what it means to wait upon the Lord for His reviving grace. Revival will come when God determines to bring it; but He calls on us to wait on Him in the interim. What does this require?

Second, we will consider the importance of setting the Lord's house in order as we wait on and begin to experience His renewing grace. Sending revival to a disorderly church is like planting a new tree in polluted soil: It will not grow as we intend. Thus, pastors and church leaders must work together to set their congregations in order before the God of new life will send His reviving rains.

Third, we will see that, for revival to flourish among us, God's people must be prepared to live sacrificially unto Him. As the Spirit of God causes the waters of grace to wash and refresh us, new people enter our churches, new needs are pressed upon the people of God, and new opportunities for service in God's Name appear. Without a spirit of sacrifice in the people of God, revival may be cut short as God's grace is bottled-up in short-sighted, self-seeking believers who have never learned to take up their cross and follow the Lord.

Finally, we will consider the necessity of preparing God's people with a vision for revival. What does it mean for individual believers and whole congregations to begin to be swept up and carried along in the flood of God's grace? How should we expect to see the glory of God magnified in our midst? Inculcating a vision for revival will help God's people to desire it more earnestly and to know what God can do in and through them during such times.

The observations and recommendations that follow are drawn from the teachings of Scripture and examples of previous generations of those who have known the reviving power of God in their midst, as well as from the author's personal experience in helping churches to prepare for God's reviving work. This book goes out with the hope that God will unite His people once again to prepare for a season of spiritual blessing such as we have never known in our generation, whether that revival comes in our lifetime, or we, through our faithful preparation under the drizzles of grace, are allowed only to become the unseen conduits of the latter rains of God's reviving mercies for the generation which follows after us.

# 1

## Waiting on the Lord

*He told them…to wait for what*
*the Father had promised.* (Acts 1.4)

Recently I saw a report about the danger of gas-heated water heaters. The report showed how such a heater, when placed in a closed room, can ignite when a volatile substance has been accidentally released, such as spilled paint or some other flammable liquid. The fumes from that liquid begin to spread out across the floor of the room where the heater stands, and build up in intensity, until they encounter the water-heater's pilot light. Then, suddenly the entire room bursts into a conflagration, with, as can be imagined, impressive results.

This is rather like the way revival comes. God has sent the awakening flame of His Holy Spirit into the Church, and, while it seems much of the time that that flame is burning as low as a mere pilot light, yet it is always present, always capable of suddenly bursting into a mighty revival fire. It only wants something to ignite, some volatile spiritual essence that it can fire with new energy and sudden power. That volatile spiritual essence is the prayers of God's people, as they seek His renewing and reviving grace without ceasing.

Seasons of revival begin in prayer, as they did at the first Pentecost, when 120 men and women joined in ongoing prayer for the promised outpouring of God's Spirit. They prayed with one mind, united in their desire to realize the promised blessings of God. They prayed continuously for ten days, and would have prayed for ten or a hundred or a thousand more, if need be. They were determined to know that promised power from on high that would send them forth as witnesses for Christ to the ends of the world. They firmly believed that all the Old Testament promises of awakening and revival were about to be fulfilled in them, and they had been commanded to 'wait' for God to work. They took this to mean that they should unite in prayer for the promises of God, and they filled that upper room and the nooks and crannies of the throne room of God's grace with fervent and effectual prayers for revival, providing a volatile spiritual essence that would ignite in the fires of Pentecost when caught up in the mighty power of the outpoured Spirit of God. As those who experienced revival during the last century observed,

> If benefits of vast magnitude are to be bestowed, they must therefore be preceded by prayers of fervid pathos; and God often delays an answer to supplication, not that he despises the anxious voice of our humble entreaty, but because *he waits till our desires gain an accession of strength, and are somewhat commensurate to the vastness of the mercy that is stored up for us*; and for this purpose he sometimes circles us with an array of troubles, that they may enhance the frequency and earnestness of our addresses to the throne of grace (emphasis added). [1]

Let God's people begin to wait on Him in prayer, to labor long and with great fervor in this most important means of preparing for revival, and revival will be just that much nearer for His Church.

From the experience of the 120, three principles emerge for such preparatory praying. I want to examine these principles and to offer some practical suggestions for beginning to apply those principles in churches today. The three principles are:

1. Those who wait on the Lord in prayer for revival must have a good understanding of what God has promised;

2. Those who wait on the Lord in prayer for revival must be devoted to the work;

3. Those who wait on the Lord in prayer for revival must follow Biblical guidelines for their prayers.

Let's look at each of these in turn.

*Understanding What God Has Promised*
The disciples had spent, in addition to three years with the Lord, an intensive period of 40 days, during which He instructed them in all things pertaining to the Kingdom of God and the coming of the Holy Spirit. How wonderful it must have been as He reviewed and explained parables He'd taught them years before; as He described the beauty and power of the Holy Spirit and reminded them of His mission of teaching, convicting, and growing the Lord's people in His grace; and as He helped them to think strategically and practically about how they would wield that power in the Kingdom that God would be establishing through their labors!

As the disciples returned from the Mount of Olives and gathered the others together for prayer, their teaching and leading, as well as their own prayers, must have been filled with Kingdom imagery and implorings of God's grace and Spirit. From them an anticipation of something new and exciting, something altogether unprecedented and only partially imaginable, must have spread out and begun to fill the hearts and inform the prayers of all present. Those who gathered in that upper room were united in their prayers; they were of one mind, committed to seeing the promise of God become reality in their midst. We can imagine that, during that 10-day period, some of the 120 had to leave for work, duties at home, and other obligations. During those times away they no doubt let their prayers return to more personal matters, although the promise of God would not have been very far from any of them. But when they were in that upper room, there was one focus, on the Kingdom and promise of God, and that focus was shaped and encouraged by the disciples, who had heard from the Lord His priorities for the latter days that were about to begin.

Pastors who would lead their churches in praying for revival need to help their people gain that singleness of focus that the 120 received from the first disciples of the Lord. They must help their members understand what revival is, how it comes, what to expect as they begin to experience it, how God's Spirit works in revival, and how He uses them to that glorious end. As Jesus taught His disciples about the Kingdom, so pastors must instruct the people entrusted to their care concerning the work of God's Spirit in revival, how He convicts lost sinners and lethargic saints, how He quickens them to new joy and hope, how He focuses their thoughts on heavenly matters and fills their conversation with spiritual delights, how He impels them into glorious service in His name and overcomes every obstacle in the way of His progress, and how He bonds them ever more firmly to one another in love:

> Every true revival begins in the church and a proof of the genuineness of the work is that it does not leave believers where they were before. They are filled with new wonder, joy, and praise, with a new sense of the privilege of serving God, and with the renewed energy that comes from being constrained by the love of Christ. What Christians had thought impossible in former years was now attempted with faith and sacrificial abandon that was to astonish the world.[2]

Churches that want to know the reviving grace of God must first be instructed in the nature and course of revival. Pastors can do this through preaching or teaching, of course, but also by reading and encouraging others to read important works on revival, such as those cited here and in John Armstrong's excellent bibliography. Pastors need to teach their elders and other leaders what to expect as revival begins to come, how to pray for revival in their homes, Bible study groups, and other ministry contexts, and how to encourage the people under their care and oversight to plead with God for revival in their times of personal devotion. They must work to shape an outlook and a passion in the hearts of God's people that leads them to believe fervently in the promise of revival and to seek above all else a fresh welling-up of God's Spirit in their midst. It falls to pastors to prepare church members for informed, vital praying for revival by teaching them what God has promised and by nurturing within them a deep hunger for Him to fulfill all His promises to all His people, all for the praise of His glorious grace.

Let pastors plan a series of sermons on periods of revival in the Scriptures – under Moses, Joshua, Nehemiah and Ezra, Josiah, and in the Book of Acts. Let them instruct the people in the teachings of Scripture concerning the Kingdom of God – the rich Old Testament imagery, the parables of the Lord Jesus, the doctrinal instruction of the apostles. And let them set forth the work of the Holy Spirit with such enthusiasm, passion, and depth that God's people will be left gasping for a fresh breath of this heavenly Wind! In our day of 'How-To' sermons, 'Feel-Good' Christianity, and man-centered faith, the people of God need their vision elevated, their desires and aspirations expanded, and their innermost longings reshaped and reformed in the forge of sound Biblical instruction.[3] No church can expect to be revived that does not know what to look and pray for. Pastors must follow the example of the Lord Jesus Christ and give their people concentrated, focused, and powerful instruction in the nature, course, and work of revival. God's people thus instructed will be much more capable of uniting in prayer for that blessed season of renewal.

### Devoted Together in Prayer
We read in Acts 1 of the people assembled in that upper room that they were *together*, that they were *of one mind*, and that they *persevered* in prayer. There is great spiritual power associated with informed saints uniting for prayer. Jonathan Edwards wrote that, before revival will come,

> There shall be given much of a spirit of prayer to God's people, in many places, disposing them to come to an express

*agreement*, unitedly to pray to God in an extraordinary manner, that he would appear for the help of his church, and in mercy to mankind, and *pour out his Spirit, revive his work*, and advance his spiritual *kingdom* in the world, as he has promised.[4]

Those days of prayer in the upper room were focused on what God had promised. The saints were of one mind in their prayers, their hearts set not on any personal needs or concerns, but wholly on the promises of God relative to the coming of His Kingdom and the work of His Spirit. How they must have encouraged and reinforced one another with their prayers! Together and continually, by some arrangement not completely explained, they besought the Lord for the promise of His Spirit and the awakening of His grace and truth with power in their midst. They were not disappointed.

They also persevered in those prayers, as we have observed. They stayed at the work of prayer until the Lord blessed and the Spirit of God ignited their prayers in power for witness and Kingdom living. This was no 'run it up the flagpole' praying; no, 'Well, let's try it for a week or so' kind of commitment. Rather, the saints in that upper room determined, like the importunate widow of Luke 18:1-8, to harass the throne of grace, to shake the walls of heaven with their pleadings, to jam the spiritual frequencies with sweet prayers and pleas, until God should give that which He had promised. Such praying – knocking, asking, seeking – brings results according to the good pleasure and the timing of God (Matt. 7:7, 8).

Pastors must call their people to prayer for revival. They must pray for it themselves, teach their people to include prayer for revival in their own prayers, and see to it that prayers for revival are part of the praying of church members in every function and activity of the congregation. They must call for special seasons of prayer for revival and make certain that they are present to lead at such times. When the people of God come together with one mind to pray for revival, and when they persevere in such praying until God opens up the windows of heaven and pours out the blessings of renewal, then they will begin to see the stirrings of God's Spirit that they seek. But Christians will not come to such earnestness and focus of prayer unless they are led there by their shepherds, who demonstrate by their own example and instruction the kind of faith that such praying requires.

*Praying God's Own Words*

We do not know exactly what the people of God prayed in that upper room. However, it is apparent that at least parts of their prayers were based on the psalms. This is no doubt what prompted Peter to interrupt their focus on prayer to lead them to the election that replaced Judas. As they were praying Psalm 109 Peter was led, by what he saw in verse 8, to have the people act at once on what he saw there.

Further, from what we see in Acts 4:23-31, God's people tended to go to the psalms for guidance in their prayers during times of crisis. There we find them drawing on Psalms 146 and 2, not only for guidance in their prayers but for the very words of those prayers as well.

This must have been the case in Acts 1 as well. Great psalms of revival – such as Psalms 5, 9, 16, 20, 27, 31, 44, 57, 67, 80, 85, and more – must certainly have provided the organization and content for the prayers of these faithful saints. How the confidence of those who prayed must have soared as they used the Lord's own words to call upon Him to fulfill His promises! How they must have grown in boldness to be praying like they had never prayed before! How their vision and hope must have grown as they were reminded of God's reviving grace in the past (Ps. 85) and assured of His promise for their own day!

We have included in this book a number of psalms that pastors can use to lead their people in prayer for revival. By following the suggested outline of these psalms pastors can structure their times of prayer more meaningfully; and by singing these psalms and using them in worship, they can begin to build prayer for revival into the daily experience and weekly worship of their people with greater effect. The great advantage in using God's own words in our prayers for revival is that we know our requests are according to His will; moreover, we will be better able to keep from straying in our focus in prayer when God's words are guiding and informing us. We will learn greater boldness and confidence in praying God's words back to Him, and we will find our own vision enlarged and our hope reinforced by the constant reminder that these are God's words, expressing God's desires and promises, and not merely our own.

### Waiting on the Lord
Dr. J. Edwin Orr has provided some very helpful suggestions concerning how to begin praying for revival in the local church. I want to summarize his guidelines, supplementing from my own experience where relevant.[5]

First, Dr. Orr suggests that pastors set a regular time for

their people to gather to pray for revival, a time when all the members of the congregation will be called together to devote themselves specifically to this kind of praying. The first Sunday morning of every month, one hour before church activities begin, might be a very good time. Other churches have found Wednesday evening or a late night on the weekend to be a good time to gather to pray for revival. Some Korean churches devote one night a week to praying all night long for the needs of the church. One hour may be enough time to start with, although it may be necessary to extend this time if the group that gathers to pray grows very large. The key is to make sure that this time is devoted exclusively to praying for revival, and that you determine to stay the course at this appointed time. Let church members unite with one mind and persevere as long as necessary until the Lord is pleased to answer their prayers and revival begins.

Second, leaders will need to provide guidance for the people in their praying. Prayer is difficult enough for most Christians. Concentrating on a single issue in prayer and devoting oneself to it for an extended period of time can be especially trying. I have already suggested that the psalms provide a rich source of guidance to help the people of God focus on revival in their prayers. At the end of this book we have provided some sample sheets that you may use to lead your people in prayer for revival. They consist of two parts. On the first side is a psalm that focuses on revival, broken down into sections that the prayer leader may use to move the people through the psalm. On the back is a versification of that psalm that can be used to sing the psalm that served as the focus of prayer for that day.

To begin the time of prayer the leader should read the

entire psalm, making some brief comments to explain its relevance to the subject of revival. The leader then reads the first section of the psalm, as it is printed on the handout, and leads the people in prayer, using the words and themes of this section as his guide. Once he has finished the people may then pray this portion of the psalm in the same way the leader did, until enough have prayed or enough time has been consumed to allow the leader to move on to the next section. People should be encouraged to keep their prayers short, so that one or two people will not dominate the entire time. Dr. Orr writes, 'It is far better to encourage people to pray for one subject at a time, in a sentence or short paragraph, joining in prayer again after others have taken part.' The people should also pray loudly enough for all to hear. This can be accomplished in several ways. You might ask those who want to pray to stand as they do. Or, place the chairs in a U-shape (if you are not in the sanctuary), so that people are facing one another as they pray. If the group is very large, assemble them in smaller groups of 4-6 so that more people can pray at the same time and more can join in with them in their prayers.

When the leader is ready, he should read the next section of the psalm and lead the people in beginning to pray it as in the first section. Continue through the entire psalm until all the sections have been prayed. The leader then closes in prayer, summarizing the major sections of the psalm as he prays. After praying through the psalm for an hour, turn the sheet over, have the people stand, and lead them in singing the words they have just prayed. Handouts can be prepared and given to the people which they may then take to their homes, Bible study groups, and Sunday school classes to use as guides in praying for revival for the remainder of the month. Encourage the people to use these guides each day and to sing the psalm together in their homes. Thus will prayers for revival be multiplied throughout the life of the congregation.

It is inevitable that prayer for revival will include times of confessing sin. The people should be reminded that the focus is on revival, and that this will include time for general confessions of sin. Other, more specific, confessions should be made only to the Lord and the offended parties. It may be a good idea to allow time for silent confession of sins to accommodate this need. The Scripture guidelines will lead in the time of general confession.

Finally, leaders should instruct the people to prepare for a long-term commitment to praying for revival. They must be encouraged to meet and meet and meet, month-in and month-out, year-in and year-out, until the heavens open and revival breezes begin to blow again. This will not be an easy challenge to sustain. People will find it difficult to believe, as revival tarries, that their prayers are having any effect. Yet they must be encouraged to persevere. They will want to give up, but leaders must encourage them to have faith and hope in the Lord's promises, so that they will stay the course of prayer until God provides that which they seek:

No great spiritual awakening has begun anywhere in the world apart from united prayer – Christians persistently praying for revival. And no awakening has endured long beyond the duration of such prayer. Have you united with like-minded Christians in agonizing, consistent prayer for revival? Until you do, it is not likely you will see the results you thirst for.[6]

Revival will come when pastors begin to lead the people in their churches to pray for it, united in their hope and vision and committed to long-term praying for the grace of God to be poured out afresh. Without such prayer we cannot expect the Lord to ignite anew the fires of spiritual awakening and renewal in our midst:

> ...*prayer, unceasing* and *earnest* is *that* wherein the great strength of a revival of religion lieth. That it is which draweth down the pure, life-giving, animating influence which sets all hearts in motion, which kindles every sacrifice, which consecrates every tongue, and makes every house a Bethel, every heart an altar and a sacrifice of sweet-smelling savor, and each body and soul a living temple, consecrated to the presence and residence of the ever-blessed Trinity.[7]

# 2

## Setting Your House in Order

*'Brethren, the Scripture had to be fulfilled...'* (Acts 1:16)

I hate selling a home. Mostly I hate it because it means you have to clean and straighten your home practically every day. No more leaving things lying around. No waiting until tomorrow to do the dishes or put the laundry away. No magazines left out on the night table. No stacks of books here, there, and everywhere. Everything has to be in order at all times, because you never know when the person will come who is going to buy your home. You want to be ready when that happens. If you want to make the sale, you have to have your house in order at all times.

It is the same with revival and the local church. As we see in Acts 1, before God would send His promised Spirit to the believers in Jerusalem, they had to take care of some unfinished business. Their house was not in order. Without proper leadership, they would not be able to care for and equip the thousands who were about to be gathered into the Body of Christ. Without an established process for identifying and appointing new leaders, the growing congregation would be hard-pressed to adjust with sufficient speed and wisdom to the changing and growing demands that would shortly be placed upon them. So, before the Spirit would be given, the people of God had to fill the office of shepherd that had been vacated by Judas.

On three other occasions, once revival had begun, the Jerusalem church was called upon to set its house in order yet again, lest the power and progress of revival should be short-circuited among them. Two of these occasions involved internal threats to the progress of the revival, and one was a threat from without. In each case, the pastoral leaders of the church took charge, leading the people of God to put His house in order so that the work of revival could continue and grow.

As we look at the apostles exercising their pastoral roles to set the church in order in Jerusalem, we will gain some insights into what is required for pastors and churches to put their own houses in order so that God will do His work of revival in their midst without delay or interruption. We will observe three pressing needs to which pastors must give attention:

1. They must lead their congregations in providing a structure and leadership for continuing health and growth.

2. They must lead their congregations in dealing with unconfessed sin.

3. They must lead their congregations in preparing to stand against any and all opposition.

## Providing a Structure and Leadership

During periods of revival a sudden awakening occurs on the part of God's people, normally coupled with a great outpouring of God's Spirit on the lost in the community.

The result is a rapid influx of new believers to the local church. As John Bonar noted during the last century, 'Viewed with respect to the church, a time of revival is a time of newness of life. Viewed with respect to the world, whether professing or openly careless, it is a time of multiplied conversions.'[1] Revival results in many new souls hungry for the sincere milk of the Word, eager to be equipped for service to the Lord, and burdened with needs which they hope the community of faith will help them to bear. God is loathe to entrust His sheep to the care of unworthy shepherds (Ezek. 34:1-10), and we can believe that He will not send revival in our churches until we have put in place the kind of leadership that is ready to shepherd, equip, and guard the flock of God for spiritual health and growth.

The church in Jerusalem took great care to make sure that qualified leaders were available for the teaching, nurture, and care of the greatly enlarged flock that God was bringing to them. Peter's leadership in providing a replacement for Judas, and the apostles' leadership in helping the people to select deacons to head off a crisis and meet the needs of a growing church (Acts 6.1-7), are examples of the kind of setting the house of God in order that allows revival to begin and to continue. Either of these situations, left unaddressed, could have throttled the revival that had begun. But because church leaders acted in a wise and timely manner in each case, the work of God's Spirit in awakening His people could go forth without interruption or hindrance.

How is it in churches today? Are the elders ready and able to shepherd the flock of God as Christ did His own disciples, personally and effectively discipling and equipping them for ministry according to His Great Commission? Are our elders sufficiently skilled in the ministry of the Word and prayer for the building-up of the Body of Christ? Is their example one of godly living and service in the name of the Lord and for the sake of His Kingdom? And are our deacons sufficiently wise, godly, trustworthy, and devoted to meeting any challenge that rapid growth might create? Are our church leaders capable of teaching the great truths of God to faithful men and women who will be brought to them through the anticipated harvest?

If the officers and other leaders of our churches are nothing more than department heads, committee chairmen, or program managers, they will not be ready to take up the work of guiding, strengthening, shepherding, and equipping for ministry that a suddenly awakened congregation will require. They must be prepared according to Biblical guidelines and criteria for the work of pastoral oversight and equipping that will ensure that their growing congregations are cared for in the grace and truth of the Lord, and that the followers of Christ are thrust out into the harvest field, no matter what their individual callings might be.

Pastors should carefully evaluate the state of their church's leadership. Are they sufficient in number and spiritual wisdom to care for a suddenly-awakened and rapidly-growing congregation? Are their houses in order, ready to cope with the fruit that a season of revival will bring? God will not send His newborn lambs to be cared for by incompetent, unmotivated, or unskilled shepherds. And He will not allow His ripened fruit to fall on unprepared ground, there simply to rot. Pastors must take the long view and begin now to prepare the leaders that tomorrow's burgeoning sheepfold will require. Elders must be equipped to serve as shepherds of God's flock, following the example that Jesus applied to Himself (1 Pet. 5:1-3; John 10). Deacons must with grace, sensitivity, and great skill prepare to address the kinds of personal needs that a diverse community should expect to encounter. And all leaders in the church must be grounded in the disciplines of Bible study, prayer, worship, evangelism, and disciple-making that will ensure a continuing flow of God's grace in and through the community of faith once revival has begun.

We may pray fervently and long for God to revive our churches, but He will not do so until we put in place the kind of leadership that will be able to care for the new life He will abundantly provide.

## Dealing with Unconfessed Sin

As in the Old Testament God required His people to deal with unconfessed sin before He would open to them the fulness of His promises (Josh. 7:8), so in the New Testament He insisted that unconfessed sin be purged from the midst of His people before the work of revival would continue. In Acts 5 a situation arose that threatened to hinder the awakening that had broken out in Jerusalem. Sin had established a presence in the house of the Lord in the persons of Ananias and Sapphira. They sinned against the Lord by lying to the Holy Spirit. He Who was graciously and powerfully advancing the Kingdom in their midst, and unloading the rich blessings of God for all, was now affronted by two people eager to divert some of His glory to themselves. They also sinned against the Body of Christ by deceiving the membership and encouraging them to heap praise on men rather than God alone, thus distracting them into a form of idolatry. The people who were observing God's blessings in their midst were being enticed to credit men for His largesse. A rock of stumbling and a stone of offense had grown up in the house of the Lord. What would the leaders of the congregation do?

The record is clear. Peter's action, under the guidance of the Holy Spirit, was no less decisive than that of Joshua and the Israelites a thousand years earlier. The judgment was severe, to be sure; but it had to be, lest men should come to believe that sin was a trivial matter or that God would not mind a bit of glory-sharing among His people.

But God was raising up a holy temple to Himself in the Body of Christ, His Church, and no place could be allowed for unconfessed sin. The result of Peter's action was that revival continued in the church, and the ministry of the apostles was greatly enhanced (Acts 5:11-14).

What is the state of church discipline in our congregations today? How earnest are we about working for the purity of Christ's Body, and about exhorting the people of God to pursue holiness in the Lord? Knowing how much the Lord despises sin, we can believe that He will not allow revival to go forward where men hold a cavalier attitude toward that which so greatly offends and angers Him. He will not entrust His sheep to the care of those who play fast and loose with rebellion (1 Sam. 15:22, 23). Without a commitment to dealing with unconfessed sins, our churches will never know the reviving breezes of God's Spirit.

Church leaders must act to teach their people about the seriousness of sin, of how much God hates it and how we are called to forego it in the pursuit of holiness. And they must expect that this will not be a popular subject, for, in our churches today, we have grown accustomed to speaking only 'positive' things to God's people. Yet pastors must not withhold sound instruction concerning the doctrine of sin and all the issues related to it. They must train their people to recognize and resist temptation; to confess their sins and seek the grace of repentance; to work for reconciliation with one another when sin has disrupted a relationship; and to join in the work of church discipline for the purity of the church and the honor of Christ. Pastors must teach their leaders how to practice church discipline, and not merely in its more negative aspects – admonition, suspension from the sacrament, and excommunication – but in its positive aspects as well – encouragement, reproof, and correction. A church that is prepared to deal with unconfessed sin is a church that is ready for revival to break out in its midst, for God is pleased to bathe His spiritual newborns in the warm graces of a pure pool, not in the stagnant waters of impurity and sin.

### Resisting Opposition

On several occasions during that first period of awakening and revival, the progress of God's work was threatened by opposition from the unbelieving world. At times, the threats were severe and accompanied by violence. At no time, however, were church leaders cowed by such a threat. They understood that, as the world had hated their Lord and Master, so it would hate them (John 15:18-19), and they were prepared to deal with such trials when they arose.

We can only speculate concerning what might have happened in Acts 4, had Peter and John returned to the people, reported the threats from the religious leaders, and advised the congregation to 'lay low' for a while. Or if they had led the believers to devote themselves to praying merely that God would, in His time, replace those ungodly leaders with ones more agreeable to the Christian cause. Or if they had organized a campaign of petitions, picketing, and political pressure to change the laws of the city more to their advantage. We cannot know what any of these courses of actions might have accomplished. But we can believe that the astonishing results described in Acts 4:31 would have been completely lacking.

Faced with the threat of persecution, the believers turned to prayer. They knew that only God could continue the work He had begun, and that they would need His protection in a special way if they were going to continue faithful in their calling to be His witnesses. They united again in prayer, using the words God Himself had provided, calling on Him to keep the work going that He had begun. And He did, in a powerful and dramatic way.

Jesus promised that those who followed Him could expect opposition from the world. But that does not excuse us from pursuing the mission He has appointed to us of proclaiming His Kingdom and calling men to repentance and faith. Paul said that persecution is the way of all who desire to live godly lives in Christ Jesus (2 Tim. 3:12). The first Christians knew such opposition and persecution, and it has been the experience of faithful believers in every generation. Are the people in our churches prepared to deal with the opposition they can expect to meet as their faith is renewed, opposition from members of their families, neighbors, school mates, and co-workers?

Pastors must take the lead in helping their people prepare for opposition and persecution. They must teach them what forms it can take – gossip, slander, being passed by for promotions, rude behavior, shunning, even violence. They must help them to see such persecution in the light of God's eternal plan, as Christ saw His own persecution on the cross (Ps. 22). Pastors must give their members a vision for the Kingdom that no amount of suffering or trial will quench, and they must teach them to deal with persecution through thanksgiving, blessing, mutual encouragement, and trust in the Lord. Above all, they must encourage their people not to shrink from persecution – not to fear men rather than God – but to stand firm in the name of Jesus, trusting in Him to accomplish His good purposes in their lives.

God will not revive a congregation merely to see it blown away by the winds of opposition. Before revival will come, pastors must make certain that the people of their congregations are prepared to deal with persecution and to persevere through it, come what may.

## Setting Your House in Order

There is nothing glamorous about this aspect of preparing for revival. Setting our houses in order doesn't generate much immediate excitement, and it can require long and sometimes tedious hours of instruction and discipling. It is an ongoing work. Yet, without it, we cannot expect God to fill our folds with new sheep. This work of setting the house in order must become the daily concern of pastors and church leaders:

> Thus what characterizes a revival is not the employment of unusual or special means but rather the extraordinary degree

of blessing attending the normal means of grace. [In previous times of revival t]here were no unusual evangelistic meetings, no special arrangements, no announcements of pending revivals. *Pastors were simply continuing in the services they had conducted for many years when the great change began* (emphasis added).[2]

We need to make certain that the 'services' we are conducting in our churches are those that will put our houses in order, making them fit nurseries for the new life that God in His reviving grace will send to them.

How, then, can we begin to set our houses in order? First, consider the state of your church's elders or other governing board (deacons, wardens, etc.). Are these folk ready to shepherd the flock of God in a responsible manner? Do they have the skills needed to disciple others? How are their interpersonal skills? Are they leading exemplary lives, the kind that others would want their children to emulate? Do they have hearts of compassion and passion for the work of God? Would they know how to equip a new believer for growth and ministry in the Lord's house? Are they fervent in their witness for Christ? If not, then you have some work to do. For God is pleased to grow His flock by entrusting them to the care of faithful shepherds. And it is the pastor's job, following the example of Jesus and Paul, to equip those shepherds for this important work.

This work must be done with a select group, using a combination of formal instruction, personal discipling, and practical guidance to help prepare them for the work of shepherding the flock of God. One place to begin would be in a study of Robert E. Coleman's classic work, *The Master Plan of Evangelism*. In this work church leaders will gain a vision for the Great Commission and an overview of the process and techniques whereby Jesus prepared His disciples for building the Church. By working together through this book, praying about and discussing practical ways to implement its teachings, pastors can help the shepherds of their churches to become better equipped to care for the fruit of revival as the Lord is pleased to bring it.

Second, the rest of the church's leadership team must also be prepared for the influx that revival will bring. Pastors must guide their leaders in developing a statement of vision for the church, one big enough to require them to trust the Lord in new and exciting ways.[3] They must teach their leaders about the nature of revival; equip them with the skills for discipling new believers that revival will require; and encourage them in their prayers and witness to greater degrees of faithfulness. Church leaders must be active in seeking revival and ready to cope with it when God is pleased to pour His blessing out on His church once again.

Finally, pastors must make sure that their leaders and congregation have a good understanding of sin and how it must be dealt with, both by individual church members and by the congregation as a whole; and they must be open and honest about the reality of opposition and persecution once their faith begins to be more visible in the larger community. Only thus will churches be ready to deal with potential obstacles to revival that may arise once the work of God's Spirit has begun in earnest.

If we want the Lord to revive our churches we must join together in one mind and seek His renewing grace in prayer. But we must also set our houses in order so that we will be able to receive and care for the new life that revival will surely bring. This does not mean that our churches must be perfect before God will revive them. It simply means that the mechanics, the people, the processes and protocols, and the vision must be in place that will provide an environment in which God's work of revival can take root and flourish. The sooner we begin to set our houses in order before the Lord, the sooner His showers of blessing will return.

# 3

# A Spirit of Sacrifice

*...and none of them claimed that anything
belonging to him was his own* (Acts 4:32).

In a time of revival God pours out great blessings upon His people, who tend to think about revival as a season of being on the *receiving end* of a renewed experience of His grace. When revival broke out among the new believers in ancient Antioch, the evidence of God's love and power was so palpable among them that Barnabas, sent by the Apostles to confirm what they were hearing, was actually able to *see* the grace of God in all its various expressions in that great city (Acts 11:23). What he saw must have mirrored his experience in Jerusalem, where hunger for the Word of God and the fellowship of believers was coupled with selflessness in giving and a power in witnessing that brought many new converts into the growing ranks of the Church (Acts 2:41-47; 4:32-37). This is what we long for in preparing for revival: A renewed and greatly heightened experience of God's presence among us in glorious grace and truth.

But it would be easy to lose sight of the fact that, during such seasons, that wonderful, life-transforming experience of God's grace not only comes *to* the people of God but is *channeled through* them to others as well. This is what Paul was thinking about when he wrote to the Corinthians about the grace of God which was 'spreading to more and more people' (2 Cor. 4:15). God reaches us with His grace through the agency of others who have also experienced that grace and touch us with His lovingkindness and truth by some Spirit-empowered word or deed. People, in other words, are the means by which other people come to know the precious grace of God. During times of revival,

> there is ample scope for the most earnest and strenuous exertions on our part, and ground enough for us to entertain feelings of very deep responsibility, regarding the manner in which we discharge the obligations resting upon us.[1]

This is all simply to say that, for revival to continue and spread, a spirit of sacrifice must exist on the part of leaders and people alike. Revival requires sacrifices of time, resources, energy, convenience, and a host of other commodities, and unless the people of God are willing and able to make such sacrifices, revival, such as it may be, will be short-lived. The grace of God is bottled up in those who have no commitment to sacrifice, so that others cannot know that grace through them.

But for God's people to be able to make those sacrifices they will need to be thoroughly prepared. Therefore, in preparing a church for revival, pastors and church leaders must begin to encourage and nurture a spirit of sacrifice among the members of the congregation, so that giving to meet the extraordinary demands and opportunities that revival can bring will actually occur and continue as long as God is pleased to visit His church with reviving breezes.

In this chapter, then, we want to examine more carefully what is required in nurturing a spirit of sacrifice as we begin to prepare our churches for revival. We will consider three points:

1. The normal Christian life requires sacrifice.

2. The need for sacrifice is greatly augmented during seasons of revival.

3. Pastors must take the lead in nurturing a spirit of sacrifice among the people of God.

*Sacrifice and the Christian Life*

The normal Christian life requires sacrifice. Believers are called to a life of giving-up, giving-away, and giving-to in order to demonstrate the self-giving love of God and meet the needs of others (John 3:16; Matt. 16:24, 25). How easy it is, in our narcissistic age, to lose sight of this most basic fact about the Christian life. We who are blessed with the saving grace of God and drawn into spiritual fellowship with Him are given every spiritual blessing, everything that we might require for whatever calling He may place before us (Eph. 1:3-14; 1 Cor. 1:4-7). His purpose in this is that we might become channels of His grace to the world. This understanding of the Christian life is as old as God's Covenant itself and was the view of the life of faith that captured the hearts and minds of believers in both Testaments (Cf. Gen. 12:1-3; Ps. 51:12, 13; 2 Cor. 4:3, 4; 1 Pet. 4.10, 11). But in our age a 'therapeutic' understanding of the life of faith has made serious inroads into many congregations, the people seeing themselves as victims of Satan's devices and the world's oppressive ways and constantly betaking themselves to this or that professional counselor, custom program, or latest spiritual insight or study/support group for some relief from their suffering. For the most part it seems, the saints of God are so busy shoring up their frail spiritual state that they have little energy, time, or inclination to give themselves away in a sacrificial manner to others. But this is what God has called us to as the *normal expression* of our new lives in Christ.

What kinds of sacrifices does the life of faith require? Consider the early Christians in Jerusalem. They sacrificed their old ways of life, including friends, routines, habitual haunts and practices, even their reputations.[2] They also sacrificed their time, setting aside leisure and other interests to join together with God's people for worship, fellowship, instruction, and ministry. They sacrificed their possessions, giving up ownership of everything as needed[3] in order to meet the needs of their brothers and sisters in Christ. Their giving and practicing fellowship together, including taking meals together in one another's homes, also required them to sacrifice a certain amount of their privacy, their convenience, and their comfort in order to follow Christ. Further we know that, in certain cases, they sacrificed their security, their homes and careers, and even their lives if devotion to Christ required. These first Christians understood and practiced what Paul commanded of all believers, that we present ourselves – all that we are and have – to the Lord as living sacrifices for His glory (Rom. 12:1, 2). They accepted sacrifice as a way of life, for they looked to the example of Jesus, who gave Himself willingly and entirely for them.

Today one could get the impression that many Christians

have forgotten how to sacrifice. Indeed, many seem to consider the Christian faith as a framework for *getting* rather than for *giving*. If the church they currently attend, or the church program in which they are currently involved, does not give them the sense of feeling good about themselves that they desire, or if it fails to please them in its worship or ministries, they will simply move on until they find one that does. The discipline of tithing has fallen by the wayside for most believers, who spend the vast majority of their income on themselves and give a portion of what's left to the work of the Lord. And every pastor is familiar with the complaint that it's hard to motivate God's people to service in His Name. We hear from every quarter that, in the Kingdom of our Lord, 20% of the people do 80% of the work, while the rest simply wait to be waited on by their leaders.

It is precisely this spiritual self-centeredness, this fundamental lack of a sense of sacrifice, that pastors and church leaders must contend with as they begin to prepare their churches for revival. Until we address and begin to reform this misconception of the life of faith we are not likely to know the reviving grace of the Lord; for revival brings with it an *increased* need for sacrifice, and, without that being central to the experience of the Lord's people prior to His renewing us, how shall we expect it to be there after?

*Sacrifice and Revival*
Revival brings an increase in the need for Christians to practice sacrifice, and that for four reasons.

First, during a season of revival, churches are faced with

greater opportunities for service. More people are coming to faith in Jesus Christ, or having their faith awakened and renewed. As those people come into the church or awaken to the true meaning of the life of faith, they will need to be discipled and cared for. Moreover, because many of them will still have ties in the unbelieving world, the change in their lives will open more doors for the work of bearing witness. Some will have to be prepared to go through those doors with those new believers and proclaim the Good News in all new settings. More people will be converted, will join the church, and will bring their full baggage of needs – physical, emotional, and spiritual – with them. Without a sense of sacrifice on the part of all believers, these needs will remain unmet, and the promise of the Gospel will turn sour in the mouths of many. In the face of these increased opportunities for ministry, will there be eager, equipped believers available and ready to say, like Isaiah, 'Here am I, Lord, send me'? Not unless we begin to equip them for sacrificial living now.

Second, during seasons of revival a greater variety of needs are presented to the church. There are needs to communicate the gospel in new ways, to counsel and advise people who are under spiritual conviction, to provide for the destitute who are coming into the church, to address the peculiar needs of new believers, and to rise to levels of financial sacrifice we have most likely not known before. Church members will need to acquire new skills in ministry. They will have to develop new ways of understanding the needs of others, and new depths of love for people in their need. It will take time and effort to discover and meet the many new needs that flow into the court of the Lord during a season of revival, and without a spirit of sacrifice on the part of church members, few will be available to give the time, effort, and resources needed to understand and address these many new needs.

Imagine, for example, what must have been required of those seven put forward to address and resolve the need which the believers in Jerusalem faced in Acts 6. These were no doubt family men, working men, with little or no experience in community service or the distribution of resources to meet the needs of strangers. Yet they stood forward when called upon, made the sacrifices necessary to learn their ministry and carry it out efficiently to the Lord's glory, thus allowing His peace to continue in His Church and the impact of the Gospel to reach the hearts of even skeptical priests. These men had learned the way of sacrifice in giving of their possessions to meet the needs of others. It only followed that they should be ready for the greater sacrifice of ongoing service to a rapidly-growing community. In the face of so many new and unfamiliar needs, will revived churches find sufficient servants who are willing to sacrifice their time, energy, and resources to meet those needs? Not unless we begin to prepare God's people for such callings now.

Third, revival brings about greater changes – in ourselves, our churches, and our communities – than we know during these torpid times. Those changes can occur rapidly, from one week to the next: New people to incorporate into the church, new neighborhoods opening up to the Gospel, new children in our Sunday schools and youth programs, new demands upon our time, talents, and treasure. These and many other changes in the church's way of life in turn create new opportunities for ministry and expose new and varied needs. Without a spirit of sacrifice widely present among the people of God, our experience of revival may fizzle rather than soar, as people react in negative ways to change and the demands that come with it.

Fourth, during a season of revival we are faced with greater pressures than normally, as is suggested by the foregoing. Churches will need to work fervently, feverishly, to keep pace with God's Spirit as He moves rapidly in their midst, creating new life, awakening dormant believers, and building the Church of the Lord Jesus Christ with wood, hay, and stubble just waiting to be transformed into gold, silver, and precious gems for the Lord's glory. There will also be opposition, both from within the ranks of the believing community as well as from without. Churches that are not experiencing revival will criticize what they see happening in revived congregations, and those criticisms will raise doubts in the minds of our church members. The local media and the hard of heart will accuse us of emotionalism, manipulation, shallowness, and sheep-stealing. God's people must be ready and able to set aside – to sacrifice – self-interest, convenience, and reputation in order to bear up under such criticism and continue to serve the needs of the believing community. Only by maintaining a spirit of sacrifice will they be able to serve as channels of God's grace to others.

Thus it should be clear that the revival we seek will require of God's people more in the way of sacrifice than they are familiar with at present. As part of preparing them for this blessed season, pastors and church leaders need to begin nurturing a spirit of sacrifice with greater devotion and urgency.

## Nurturing a Spirit of Sacrifice

What, then, can pastors and church leaders do?

I might suggest four practical steps for nurturing a spirit of sacrifice among the people of God. First, pastors and church leaders must make sure that their own example is one of sacrifice. The shepherds of God's flock instruct the sheep under their care as much by their lives as by their words (1 Pet. 5:1-3). Unless their lives demonstrate the living sacrifice to which God calls all His people, they can not expect the people in their care to attain it.

This is not to suggest that pastors and church leaders should parade their extraordinary service and sacrifice before the congregation and the community. Sacrifice must not become a reason for boasting on the part of church leaders. Rather, let them develop a healthy work ethic in the Lord's service; let them be the first to step forward when new needs emerge; let them be diligent in all aspects of their callings and available as the Lord leads, even to the humblest of God's people or callings. Let them increase their spiritual disciplines and their outreach of love to needy people. Let them be zealous for the work of evangelism and disciple-making, beginning in their own homes. Let them, in other words, show by their example that the work of the Kingdom of God has the highest priority in all their affairs, and others will certainly take note and begin to emulate their example. As people who have 'devoted themselves to the ministry of the saints' (1 Cor. 16:15) church leaders must let their example of sacrifice be the hallmark by which they are known among the people they serve.

Second, church leaders must lead and encourage the members of their churches in practicing the sacrifice of thanksgiving (Ps. 50:14, 15, 23). As demands on people grow – as they surely will during a season of revival – a tendency for grumbling and complaining may arise. Who are all these new people? Why do they all have to come here? Why are we spending so much time, giving so many of our resources, and allotting so much of our facility to accommodating them? Why do they keep calling on me to help? Yet God commands us to give thanks in every circumstance, in every situation (1 Thess. 5:18). Whether we feel thankful or not is irrelevant; we do not live by feeling, but by faith and obedience. Pastors and church leaders who demonstrate a lifestyle of thanksgiving, and who teach that practice to their church members, will lay down in their churches a foundation for sacrificial living upon which they can build for the future. Instead of allowing God's people to worry and complain, let them be taught to give thanks, no matter how painful the experience of giving thanks may be, especially when one has been wronged, deprived of some good, or pushed beyond what seems reasonable. Sacrifice begins in the heart, and a heart disciplined to give thanks in the face of every situation will be more likely to engender other kinds of sacrifice as new needs and opportunities arise.

But God's people must be taught this discipline, for it will seem strange to them. Too often we associate giving thanks with feeling thankful, as I have suggested above, and we can believe that giving thanks without the associated feeling is somehow hypocritical. To the contrary, *giving* thanks is simply being obedient; *feeling thankful* will follow as we watch the Lord unfold His hidden goodness to those who love Him and are called according to His purpose (Rom. 8:28). By giving thanks as an act of faith we sacrifice all need fully to understand what has happened to us, all desire for vengeance, redress, or reward, and all self-indulgent worry and fear. Instead, we give thanks as an act of obedience to our sovereign and loving Lord, and trust in Him to work out His good pleasure in our lives. When God's people have begun to practice the sacrifice of thanksgiving in the normal course of their daily lives, they will be much better prepared for the larger sacrifices that revival will most certainly require.

Third, pastors and church leaders must recover the discipline of fasting and lead their congregations in the same. These days, when spiritual disciplines as a whole are lagging among the people of God, the discipline of fasting is almost unheard of, except among an extraordinary few. Yet the example of saints in both Testaments, as well as throughout the course of Church history, is that fasting must be part of the believer's normal routine of strengthening fellowship with and dependence on the Lord. Jesus, after all, did not say, '*if* you fast,' but '*when* you fast' (Matt. 6:16). He assumed that His followers would fall in line with the great tradition of God's Covenant people and practice the discipline of fasting as a normal part of spiritual growth and preparation for ministry.

Here is not the place for a lengthy elaboration on this important practice. Suffice it to say that fasting is excellent training for a life of sacrifice. When we fast we discipline our bodies, minds, and spirits to give up precious material necessities in order that we may concentrate on spiritual truths. When the pains and pangs of hunger remind us that we are frail creatures of flesh, we cry out to the Lord to sustain and strengthen us, and we find His grace sufficient for our weakness and need. The sacrifice of material necessities in order to concentrate on the Lord and His good and perfect will is all that is required in *any* form of sacrifice; thus, fasting can be a wonderful discipline to prepare us for the sacrifices required in our daily lives as believers, as well as for the greater sacrifices that we will be presented with during seasons of revival.

Pastors and church leaders should undertake a careful study of this discipline and begin its discreet practice, gradually teaching and leading others in the practice of fasting as well. This will go a long way toward nurturing a spirit of sacrifice among the people of God.

Finally, pastors and church leaders must challenge every member of their churches to engage in meaningful, sacrificial ministry *now*. If people in our churches are content merely to ride the pews; if we seldom see new leaders arising from our congregation; if our programs go wanting for people to lead and direct them; and if we are failing to reach out to the lost and needy in the neighborhoods around us, it can only be because pastors and church leaders have not motivated, equipped, challenged, and led their congregations to meaningful, sacrificial ministry. I do not mean to suggest that everyone in the church needs to join or start some program of ministry; rather, pastors and church leaders should begin teaching them to discover the opportunities for ministry – doing good and speaking God's Word – with the people around them. Church members are surrounded by needy people – in their neighborhoods, schools, workplaces, in the larger community where they shop and play, and in their various social and professional contexts. Here there are lonely, lost, or unloved people to whom the grace of God could begin to flow if the people of God could only learn to reach out to them as He did to us. If we challenge and equip God's people for such a way of life, they will quickly learn to sacrifice in all the various ways we have described in order to show the love of God to the people they see each day. This will prepare them for the greater sacrifices that revival will demand.

But God's people will not come to this kind of lifestyle on their own. They must be challenged and equipped for it, and it is the duty of pastors and church leaders to prepare God's people for works of ministry and to lead them into them (Eph. 4:11, 12).

Without a spirit of sacrifice the people of God will not be ready to assume the greater challenges and responsibilities that arise during seasons of revival. God may be holding back His renewing grace until He sees in us that willingness to sacrifice that will allow His grace to flow freely and powerfully to all around us, then once again His Spirit will begin to stir in our midst. Now is the time for pastors and church leaders to begin nurturing and developing this spirit of sacrifice in the people under their care, as yet another way of preparing our churches for revival.

# 4

## A Vision for Revival

*'Behold, I see the heavens opened, and the Son of Man
standing on the right hand of God'*
(Acts 7.56).

### To See as Alexander

When, suddenly, he turns that fearsome horse
to face the sun, and swings himself upon
its unridden back, to the astonishment
of all, they see a brash young prince, of course,
and are mildly amused. His father hopes, no doubt,
that he might one day prove himself to be
an able king of Macedon, like he
himself has tried to be. He might work out
after all, his diminutive stature not-
withstanding. His tutor, Aristotle, longs
to see the day when this impetuous, strong-
willed lad will master all that he has taught.
But he, upon that mighty stallion, sees
all Persia bowed, and India on its knees.

There is a growing body of literature discussing the important
role of vision in human life.[1] People are greatly influenced
in their daily choices and activities by how they see
themselves, what their hopes and dreams are, and what they

believe to be possible for their lives. This is as true for Christians as for all other people. Everyone holds in mind some vision for his life, and that vision plays a powerful role in determining the kind of life each person will live.

Sadly, for many Christians, their vision is much like that of the amused courtiers in the poem above. Their vision consists of performing their daily duties and trying to find some enjoyment in their lives. They go to work, tend to their families, participate in their churches according to their interests or needs, and seek enjoyment in friends, cultural activities, and other kinds of diversions. A good day for such people is one in which all these basic components of their personal vision – which is largely unarticulated – realize some satisfaction. Others have a vision more like King Philip, or Aristotle, one that is more thoughtfully considered. They pursue larger interests and take on greater responsibilities because they nurture a vision of their lives as influencing and reaching other people, perhaps even, beyond their own lifetimes. Their vision leads them to work harder than most and to develop plans and means for helping to ensure that their endeavors will not die with them. Many pastors and church leaders have a vision like this.

But very few Christians seem to have a vision like that of Alexander, who could see beyond the limitations of youth, stature, time, distance, and physical and political possibility to a world made subject to his rule. Yet this is precisely the kind of vision that the Scriptures call all believers to maintain, a vision which sees themselves growing in grace and realizing virtually unlimited power to serve the King of Kings; a vision which holds in their minds a picture of a world that is being progressively subdued to the rule of Jesus

Christ; a vision of themselves as warriors in an invincible army that goes forth in the name of an all-powerful Sovereign to turn the world upside down for His glory (2 Pet. 3:18; 2 Cor. 10:3-5; 1 Pet. 2:9, 10; Eph. 3:20; etc.).

There are perhaps many reasons why the vision of today's Christians is, on the whole, so shallow and lacking in power. The distractions of everyday life, the generally unbelieving and secular tenor of the contemporary consensus, fear of what they may have to give up, fear of men, and lack of proper instruction all might be cited as explanations for our failure of vision. In the end, however, these all come down to one thing: unbelief. Either we know what the Scriptures teach concerning how we ought to see ourselves, our mission, and our individual callings, and we simply do not believe what we read, or we have not been exposed to such Scriptural teaching and lack the faith for such a vision because of our ignorance of the whole counsel of God.

Without addressing this matter of the Christian's vision, it is unlikely that we will know revival. For such a vision requires faith to believe God's Word and a willingness to order all one's affairs according to the promises held out therein concerning our callings in life. Pastors and church leaders who want to prepare their churches for revival will have to address the vision their congregations entertain, for themselves, for their churches and the Church as a whole, and for the greater glory of God. In this chapter we will address the question of vision. In particular, we will consider:

1. The believer must be encouraged to nurture a vision of himself as a servant of God who is called to glorify Him in every area of his life.

2. The local church must have a vision of itself as a community in mission which God is raising up to bring great glory and honor to Himself.

3. The church must cultivate a growing vision of the glory of God in His holiness, majesty, power, and delight in His people.

The story of Stephen gives us ample opportunity to consider each of these aspects of vision, for without a vision of himself revived and part of a revived community involved in the business of the eternal King, and in which that King of heaven and earth takes great pleasure and delight, it is unlikely he would have been able to give the witness to the risen Lord which we find in Acts 7.

*The Believer's Vision*
The man we encounter in Acts 6 and 7, selflessly serving the needs of the church and testifying boldly before the religious leaders of his day, strikes us as an unusual person. We do not see many such people today, people with such a depth of Biblical knowledge and understanding, the boldness to proclaim their faith before the most hostile of audiences, the courage of their convictions in the face of death, and a compelling sense of the transcendent world that sustains them in all things. In a certain sense it is true that Stephen was an unusual man, in that he stood out among his fellow believers as one with a good reputation, great wisdom and spirituality, and strong faith in God. Because of these attributes he was appointed to serve the congregation in Jerusalem at a time of crisis, and his ministry proved to be

most effective (Acts 6:1-7). He was also unusual in that the Lord was pleased, following his service in Jerusalem, to set him apart for additional, broader ministries associated with the preaching of the gospel and the progress of the Kingdom of God (Acts 6:8ff.). It was as he served in this capacity that he came to the attention of the Sanhedrin and was brought before them to give an account of his preaching. He was in many ways a man head and shoulders above his peers, an unusual man among the followers of Christ.

On the other hand, Stephen was not all that unusual from the rest of his brethren, in that, prior to his calling as deacon, he was a lay person, perhaps with a family, undoubtedly with some kind of work that occupied a significant portion of his time, and no doubt having other interests and responsibilities as well. He was the beneficiary of no more special training or preparation than the other members of the Jerusalem congregation – no seminary or Bible college, or anything like that. He simply rose above the other members of his congregation in learning, piety, devotion, and service as a result of his growth in the Lord and because of his vision of the Lord's calling on his life. While we do not have any explicit record of Stephen's personal vision, we can, I believe, deduce from his life and ministry something of what that vision must have been.

Two aspects of Stephen's personal vision are particularly relevant for our concern. The first is his evident sense of the Christian life as an arena of ever-increasing service to the glory of God and for the edification of the Church. For Stephen, to be a follower of Christ was to be called to serve, as Christ Himself had come to serve (Mark 10:42-44). This explains the eagerness and care with which he evidently attended to the apostles' teaching. A cursory reading of Stephen's defense before the Sanhedrin reveals a depth of Biblical understanding that escapes many contemporary pastors, let alone lay men and women. Stephen was called to serve, and, since it is the Word of God that equips us for every good work, he knew he must pay special attention to what he was taught if he would be ready for whatever service God might set before him. We can imagine him faithfully in attendance at every opportunity to hear the Word of God proclaimed and taught; carefully and eagerly listening to every point of doctrine; diligently reviewing and applying in his life what he had heard; and adding to his store of Biblical understanding each day. How he must have hungered for the Word of God! Oh, that his vision of the life of service, and his understanding of the role of Scripture in preparing us for that life, might grip the hearts and minds of more church members today.

Stephen's sense of the Christian life as one of service to God's people may also help to account for his extraordinary piety. We read that Stephen was a man of good reputation, full of the Spirit and wisdom, as well as of grace and power (Acts 6:3, 5, 8). He had the face of an angel as he stood before his accusers (Acts 6:15). Truly he stood out among his contemporaries as one who walked with the Lord. Such piety does not come automatically, as it were; rather a man must struggle against sin, fight against temptation, labor to lay aside the old man and put on the new, and let the Word of God dwell in Him richly with life-transforming power before he begins to grow in grace like Stephen. Effective service requires deep faith in God, a demeanor of grace and truth, and the power of God's Spirit, the hallmarks of

Christian piety; and only a vision of one's calling in Christ as a life of service to others will bring forth devotion to attaining such piety by God's grace. Stephen had such a vision; may pastors and church leaders infuse that same vision into the members of their congregations as we prepare for the reviving visitation of God.

Stephen's personal vision also accounts for his readiness to step forward in the service of the Lord with ever-increasing responsibility. His ministry must have begun with those around him, in his family and among his friends and associates. They, having experienced the grace of God in him, and hearing the Word of God from him, put him forward at a time of crisis as one fitted to serve the needs of the larger community. His effectiveness in that role saw him being drawn into evangelism and apologetics among the people of Jerusalem. From there he was elevated to the supreme calling of service as a martyr for the cause of Christ. His life unfolded according to his vision. So it will be with us. Only may our vision be more like that of Stephen, as one of serving others for the glory of God and the edification of His Church.

The second relevant aspect of Stephen's personal vision may be more concisely summarized. This relates to his having been called to a life of transcendent loyalty above all. For Stephen nothing was clearer, and nothing more important, than that he should spend his life in humble obedience to the risen Christ. No temporal obligations, worldly diversions, or relational responsibilities were allowed to get in the way of his running the race set before him, his eyes firmly and unflinchingly set on Christ. This explains his boldness and directness before the men of

Jerusalem and the Sanhedrin. No amount of intimidation or threat could cause him to hold back or to compromise his witness for Christ. It also accounts for his readiness to lay down his life for the Gospel. Stephen surely must have known at least what *could* result from his interrogation by the religious leaders. Yet he held back nothing of his witness for Christ. When martyrdom became his lot, we see him willingly and graciously following in the footsteps of his Lord. It also explains his confidence in the Lord's mercy, as revealed in his glimpse into the heavens, where King Jesus stood to welcome His faithful champion home.

How many Christians do you know today with this kind of vision of the life to which they have been called in Christ? Yet if we are to know revival, we shall have to nurture just such a vision among the members of the congregations under our care. For sustained revival to break out among the Lord's people today, they shall have to cultivate a vision like Stephen's, of loving service and transcendent loyalty to the risen Christ.

## The Church's Vision

It is one thing for church members to nurture a proper vision of their lives in Christ. It is quite another thing for that vision to be translated to an entire congregation and to become the bond which unites them as a community of God's people.

We may note two aspects of the vision which guided the church in Jerusalem – Stephen's church - and which served to define their sense of identity and mission. First, this rapidly-growing group of people seems clearly to have understood that they were called to be a community together of the followers of Christ. We see this in their dedication to being together for times of instruction, even to the point of opening their homes for the ministry of the Word. Those who study and learn together are more likely to grow and serve together according to the same vision of the Christian life and the mission of the Church. We see it also in their readiness to share with one another according to the needs of the moment. And we see it in their devotion to maintaining their sense of community, even the face of racial and economic disparities, and amid the continuing influx of new members.

How unlike the vision of so many churches today! In most congregations church attendance rarely is as great as the number of people on the roll. Sunday school is grossly under-attended, as are Sunday night services and mid-week Bible studies. There is little sense of urgency on the part of churches today concerning the necessity of studying God's Word together. Ministries designed to address the spiritual and physical needs of church members go wanting for resources and personnel. Church members seem hardly to know one another, much less care for one another. And churches today are more likely to split over difficult issues than to seek ways of reconciling with one another and maintaining the unity of the Spirit in the bond of peace.

This situation is a commentary on the kind of corporate vision churches are allowed to hold. We will not know true and lasting revival while such smallness of vision obtains among us.

The Jerusalem church also saw itself as called to press on in pursuit of the interests and expansion of the Kingdom of God. This explains not only their ministries to one another and their constant witness in the community, but also their response to the situation involving Ananias and Sapphira, as well as their readiness to leave all for the cause of the Gospel. The calling to follow Jesus in self-giving and witness had taken over this entire congregation. They had experienced true *metanoia*, that change of mind and heart which comes with saving faith to begin the process of making all things new in our lives. Old loyalties had passed away. These people were committed to Christ and the progress of His Kingdom, come what may. Each in his or her own way had laid hold on the vision that Stephen embraced, and all of them together sustained a corporate vision of Kingdom expansion unto the ends of the earth.

Where does such vision exist today among the churches of the Lord? Too often one gets the impression that local churches want to be hospitals and rest homes for the saints, rather than mighty armies equipped for battle in the Name of the King. To the extent that this is so it can only be because pastors and church leaders have allowed and encouraged it. They also must be the ones who begin to instill a different, more Biblical vision in the minds of their congregations. If we are going to know revival our churches must bristle with the same kind of Kingdom anticipation which filled that upper room in the days before Pentecost and for generations thereafter.

### The Vision of God in His Glory

Overarching and undergirding both Stephen's vision and that of the church he served were certain fundamental convictions concerning the glory of God. This vision of God in His glory was the driving force, the irresistible motivation in all their activities. We see it, for example, in their conviction of the absolute certainty and utter reliability of God's redeeming plan. His Kingdom had come, and IIis will would now be done on earth, just as it is in heaven. Stephen may die a martyr, but the Gospel must be proclaimed. Church members may lose their homes and property and be separated from work, family, and friends, but the proclamation of the Good News must go forward. The King was going forth conquering and to conquer for the greater glory of God, and these first Christians would allow nothing to keep them from serving that end as well.

They also must have kept in their minds a vision of Christ exalted to the Father's right hand, subduing all His enemies, delighting in His people, and making ready to bring them to Himself. Peter and the other apostles had clearly proclaimed it; the people had claimed His power in their prayers and come to know the reality of it in their life together; and so it is little wonder that, at the moment of his great need, that mental vision became a spiritual, and in some way, a visual reality for Stephen. How different this vision of Christ ruling at the Father's right hand is from the way we often think of Jesus today. And how important it is that believers begin again to recover this glorious vision (Col. 3:1-3).

## Developing Christian Vision

Part of preparing our churches for revival is nurturing in them the kinds of expectations and anticipation that enable the Spirit to work rapidly, uninterruptedly, and with great effect once His work of revival has begun. This gets to the matter of vision. What hopes, what aspirations, what mental images do our people entertain, and is their vision consistent with what the Scriptures prescribe? How can pastors and church leaders begin to shape and expand the vision of church members and of the congregation as a whole?

We must begin with ourselves. What vision of the life of faith do we hold? Is it broad and expansive, sacrificial and self-giving, bold and daring and infused with a longing for the glory of God? Pastors and church leaders need to examine their personal vision, meditating long on the Word of God, nurturing images of the promises of God in full outworking in their lives, and articulating a personal vision that is faithful to the whole counsel of God. Ask God to give you a vision like Stephen's or Paul's or even that of the Lord Jesus. Let the teaching about God's Kingdom so inform your outlook, hopes, and dreams that you begin to set goals that will take you far beyond anywhere you've ever been before in your walk with and service to the Lord. Settle into a new vision of your life, and let that vision lead you to see beyond previous experience or perceived limitations to a time of glorious new beginnings and significant achievement for the glory of God.

Then begin to let that vision come through in your teaching, preaching, discipling, and all other aspects of your life and ministry. The members of your congregation are not likely to grow beyond the vision that you hold for your own life in Christ. Nor are they likely to rise above their current vision into greater and more glorious vistas of possibility unless pastors and church leaders set a deliberate course of teaching and leading. Each sermon, Bible class, discipleship meeting, leadership training activity, counseling session, and committee or board meeting must include some aspect of vision-casting, until the people of God begin to see themselves, their church, and their calling from the Lord in an altogether different light. Think of the many times, and the many different ways, that Jesus held the vision of the Kingdom of God out for His disciples. He lavished upon them parables, analogies, straightforward teaching, and a consistent example of the Kingdom, then reinforced that with 40 days of solid instruction on the Kingdom of God prior to His ascension. No wonder they were filled with such eager – albeit misshapen – anticipation of that vision just before He left them (Acts 1:1-7). Their vision grew and expanded as the Lord taught and led them. So it must be among the members of our churches as we work to prepare them for the reviving grace of God.

*Conclusion*
God is preparing to revive His churches, as He has done so often in the past. *And He will do it!* But will He do it in *our* churches? While we acknowledge the absolute sovereignty of God in the bestowing of His renewing mercies, still, we must not neglect our responsibility in preparing our people for what God wants to do among us. Through careful instruction, earnest prayer, diligence in setting our house in order, learning the ways of sacrifice, and nurturing a proper vision of the Christian life, pastors and church leaders can help prepare their congregations as ready vessels for the reviving and spreading grace of God. May we be diligent in so doing, until God is pleased to rain down His sweet renewing blessings upon us once again.

# Afterword:

## Leading the Way

*On your walls, O Jerusalem, I have appointed watchmen, and all night they will never keep silent* (Isa. 62:6, 7).

It has been the burden of this little book to argue that God can and will revive His Church, as He has done so often in the past, when it pleases Him to cause the blessed rains of renewing grace to fall down upon us once again; and to insist that, while we cannot manipulate God into reviving us, yet we can take certain steps to prepare our churches for the coming season of renewal. If, in faith, pastors and church leaders will begin to demonstrate to God, in the ways we have suggested, that they are eager and ready for revival, it may please Him to bring renewal sooner than later. Revival, though it appears to come suddenly and unexpectedly, actually begins in the hearts of God's people as they turn to Him in the ways we have suggested and begin to open channels for His renewing grace to flow to and through them once again.

Yet for revival to be something more than just the awakening of one congregation, ministers and church leaders will have to work together across a broad spectrum of denominations, beginning with the work of prayer. During the great revivals of the past, pastors from Christ-loving churches of all denominations joined faithfully to pray for the outpouring of God's Spirit. Setting aside their differences and concentrating on what they have in common, as well as what they jointly seek, they have managed to forge strong bonds in prayer that God has been pleased to honor with the latter rains of renewal. Moreover, once revival began, it was often the case that these ministers continued praying together, beseeching God to extend His renewing grace to more and more people:

> These men were united in the belief that God has appointed the means of prayer and preaching for the spread of the gospel and that these are *the great means* in the use of which he requires churches to be faithful....Exclusive attention to denominational interests may prevail among Christians in a period of spiritual decline; it never does so in days of enlarged blessing.[1]

Every pastor and church leader has his list of reasons why uniting with other pastors and church leaders has not been a priority – or even an aspect – of his ministry: Too much to do in my own ministry. Theological differences. Never met the fellow. It's too hard to get started and not likely to last. And so on. Most of these, however, boil down to one underlying explanation for our lack of commitment to praying together: We just do not believe that God regards our prayers for revival. It is a problem of unbelief, nothing more.

But here is what God says to the watchmen He has appointed over His churches:

> 'On your walls, O Jerusalem, I have appointed watchmen; all day and all night they will never keep silent. You who remind the Lord, take no rest for yourselves; and give Him no rest until He establishes and makes Jerusalem a praise in the earth' (Isa. 62:6, 7).

The overseers whom God has appointed to care for His people are called to remind Him constantly of what He has promised to do for His Church. They sacrifice their own convenience and rest in order to fulfill this duty. They besiege His throne of grace relentlessly and together, with the fervent prayer that God might pour out His blessings on the Church and turn her again to be a blessing and a praise in the earth. This is a task that they perform *together*, undivided by any differences of Christian maturity, fine points of doctrine, style of worship, philosophy of ministry, liturgical dress, sacramental practice, or any other thing, and united only in their belief that God, Who gave His Son for the redemption and ingathering of His Church, will do what He has promised in response to their prayers:

> ...prayer that throws believers in heartfelt need on God, with concern for the salvation of sinners, will not go unanswered. Prayer of this kind precedes blessing, not because of any necessary cause and effect, but because such prayer secures an acknowledgment of the true Author of the blessing. And where such a spirit of prayer exists, it is a sign that God is already intervening to advance his cause.[2]

## Begin with Yourself

United prayer for revival must begin first of all in personal prayer. If pastors and church leaders do not believe enough in the need for revival and the promise of God to bring it, they will not devote much time to beseeching His throne of grace for it. On the other hand, as revival becomes a consuming passion, they will find that they are never very far away from praying God to bring it soon.

Let each of us examine ourselves. How much do we really

understand about revival, about the promises God has made and the ways He has delivered on those promises in the past? How earnestly and sincerely do we long for revival, ache and yearn for it? Is prayer for revival part of our own prayers each day? Are we never very far from turning to the Lord on behalf of a renewed stirring of his Spirit among the people under our care? As we begin to make prayer for revival a more fervent and consistent element of our own prayers we will find a growing desire to enter into such prayer with others as well.

## Praying with Others

As each pastor and church leader begins to prepare his own church for revival, let him look for another pastor or leader in another congregation with whom to begin uniting in prayer. Do not consider it a light thing that your efforts at bringing revival to the Lord's people throughout your community should begin in such a small way:

> It has been remarked, as an important and encouraging fact in the history of the revivals with which we are best acquainted, that the moving spring of them all has been *prayer – believing, earnest, united* – by a smaller number; it has been by only a very few at first, but, immediately preceding the remarkable awakenings, by a greater number of Christians, as on sacramental occasions.[3]

Begin with another pastor or church leader; later you may add another, then others. God will grow your group as you show yourselves faithful to keep the appointed time of prayer and the focus on revival, even if it is weeks or months or *years* before the blessings of God begin to fall once again.

In this respect pastors and church leaders must resolve that they will continue to pray together for revival in the full knowledge that it may not please God to bring revival in their generation. Their prayers may only lay a foundation, establish a pattern for others to follow, and cut the channels through which God's reviving grace will flow in some future generation. We must be content with this before we unite to pray, or we will not be able to keep up the work of prayer in the face of a perceived lack of response on God's part. Calvin wrote:

> Understand, moreover, that if he delays to grant the desire of his children, and does not immediately manifest himself in the time of need for their deliverance, it is generally because he wishes to stir them up and urge them on to supplicate his favour.[4]

When you are together with other pastors and church leaders to pray for revival, make certain that this is your only focus. Do not let ministry or personal needs, upcoming events, or theological issues intrude into this most important work. There are other times when you can gather to devote attention to such matters. Devote this time to the business of praying for revival. Let the prayer guides that follow in the Appendix help to keep you on track. Read from the promises of God concerning revival. Pray His Words back to Him from the psalms and elsewhere, calling upon Him, like faithful and earnest watchmen, to be faithful to what He has promised. In your prayers rehearse the mighty works of God from previous seasons of revival, as we see exemplified in Psalm 85. This will encourage all in attendance to keep seeking the renewing blessings of the

Lord. Sing precious hymns of revival, joining hands to pray and praise the Lord as He leads.

Only be united before Him in prayer, and you will find your own zeal for revival growing stronger, and your resolve to lead your church in preparing for revival becoming much firmer and more enthusiastic. Keep the work of praying together going, faithfully meeting at the appointed time as though it were the most important time of the week or month. Let nothing short of personal emergency or ministry crisis or other unavoidable business keep you from this appointment to stand together on the walls to call down the blessings of God on His people. When the servants of God begin to lay aside their differences and unite in heart, soul, mind, and strength in the work of praying for revival, a fresh fluttering of the heavenly Dove and great downpours of divine grace cannot be far behind.

# Appendix

## Revival Prayer Guides

The prayer guides that follow can be used for personal or group worship to promote praying for revival. Their use is explained in chapter 1. Readers may reproduce these pages in any form as needed.

I have left space on the front of each guide so that, as the leader reads through and gives a brief explanation of the psalm, listeners can make notes of items they would like to remember in prayer.

# Psalm 13

*vv. 1, 2: The people of God cry out to Him in their separation.*
How long wilt Thou forget me, O Lord? For ever? How long
wilt Thou hide Thy face from me? How long shall I take counsel
in my soul, having sorrow in my heart daily? How long shall
mine enemy be exalted over me?

*vv. 3, 4: They beseech the Lord to hear their earnest cries.*
Consider and hear me, O Lord my God: lighten mine eyes,
lest I sleep the sleep of death; lest mine enemy say, I have
prevailed against him; and those that trouble me rejoice when I
am moved.

*vv. 5, 6: The people look to God to deliver and restore them.*
But I have trusted in Thy mercy; my heart shall rejoice in Thy
salvation. I will sing unto the Lord, because He hath dealt
bountifully with me.

## Psalm 13
Tune: Finlandia ('Be Still, My Soul')

How long, O Lord,
how long will You forget me?
How long will You Your face conceal from me?
How long must I take counsel in my spirit,
and sorrow fill my heart throughout the day?
How long, O Lord, shall my opponent triumph?
O Lord my God,
please hear me as I pray.

Consider, Lord, and answer me, my God;
my eyes enlighten
lest I sleep as dead;
lest he who hates me boast that he has triumphed,
and go rejoicing
while I shaken stay.
How long, O Lord, shall my opponent triumph?
O Lord my God,
please hear me as I pray.

But I have trusted in Your lovingkindness!
My heart rejoices in Your saving grace!
To You I sing because You've greatly blessed me;
so bountiful Your mercies unto me!
No more, O Lord, shall my opponent triumph,
for by Your grace revival I shall see!

# Psalm 25

*vv. 1-3: The people cast themselves entirely on the mercy of God.*

Unto Thee, O Lord, do I lift up my soul. O my God, I trust in Thee: Let me not be ashamed, let not mine enemies triumph over me. Yea, let none that wait on Thee be ashamed: Let them be ashamed which transgress Thy cause.

*vv. 4 and 5: They cry out to God for guidance in their time of need.*

Shew me Thy ways, O Lord; teach me Thy paths. Lead me in Thy truth, and teach me; for Thou art the God of my salvation: On Thee do I wait all the day.

*vv. 6-11: They appeal to the Lord's mercy to deliver them from their sin.*

Remember, O Lord, Thy tender mercies and Thy lovingkindnesses; for they have been ever of old. Remember not the sins of my youth, nor my transgressions; according to Thy mercy remember Thou me for Thy goodness' sake, O Lord. Good and upright is the Lord: Therefore will He teach sinners in the way. The meek will He guide in judgment; and the meek will He teach His way. All the paths of the Lord are mercy and truth unto such as keep His Covenant and His testimonies. For Thy Name's sake, O Lord, pardon mine iniquity; for it is great.

*vv. 12-19: In their weakness the people look to the Lord for help against their enemies.*

What man is he that feareth the Lord? Him shall He teach in the way that He shall choose. His soul shall dwell at ease; and his seed shall inherit the earth. The secret of the Lord is with them that fear Him; and He will shew them His Covenant. Mine eyes are ever toward the Lord; for He shall pluck my feet out of the net. Turn Thee unto me, and have mercy upon me; for I am desolate and afflicted. The troubles of my heart are enlarged: O bring Thou me out of my distresses. Look upon mine affliction and my pain; and forgive all my sins. Consider mine enemies; for they are many; and they hate me with cruel hatred.

*vv. 20-22: The people call upon the Lord to renew them.*

O keep my soul, and deliver me: Let me not be ashamed; for I put my trust in Thee. Let integrity and uprightness preserve me; for I wait on Thee. Redeem Israel, O God, out of all his troubles.

## Psalm 25 (vv. 1-9, 12, 13, 16)
### Tune: St. Petersburg ('My Hope is Built On Nothing Less')

To You, O Lord, I lift up my soul:
In You I trust, My God alone.
O let me not ashamed be,
Nor let my foes exult over me.
> *Refrain*
> To me be gracious, Lord, and turn,
> For I am lonely, sad, and worn.

Make me, O Lord, Your pathways to know.
And show me the way that I should go.
Teach me Your truth, O Savior, I pray;
For on You I wait throughout the day.
> *Refrain*

Remember, Lord, Your kindness and grace;
Keep not my sins before Your face.
Your lovingkindness, O let it be
How You blessed Lord remember me.
> *Refrain*

All good and upright is the Lord;
Thus sinners He teaches from His Word.
In justice He the meek shall lead;
The humble He with His truth shall feed.
> *Refrain*

O who is he who fears the Lord?
May God instruct Him from his Word!
And let his soul in riches abide,
His children forever at his side.
> *Refrain*

# Psalm 28

*vv. 1, 2: The people cry out to God with one voice to hear them.*

Unto Thee I will cry, O Lord, my Rock; be not silent to me; lest, if Thou be silent to me, I become like them that go down into the pit. Hear the voice of my supplications, when I cry unto Thee, when I lift up my hands toward Thy holy oracle.

*vv. 3-5: The people seek help in dealing with wickedness.*

Draw me not away with the wicked, and with the workers of iniquity, which speak peace to their neighbours, but mischief is in their hearts. Give them according to their deeds, and according to the wickedness of their endeavours: Give them after the work of their hands; render to them their desert. Because they regard not the works of the Lord, nor the operation of His hands, He shall destroy them, and not build them up.

*vv. 6-8: They testify of their trust in the Lord and His strength.*

Blessed be the Lord, because He hath heard the voice of my supplications. The Lord is my strength and my shield; my heart trusted in Him, and I am helped: Therefore my heart greatly rejoiceth; and with my song will I praise Him. The Lord is their strength, and He is the saving strength of His anointed.

*v. 9: The people cry out to God for salvation and renewal.*

Save Thy people, and bless Thine inheritance: Feed them also, and lift them up forever.

## Psalm 28
### Tune: He Leadeth Me

To Thee, O Lord, my Rock I call:
Do not be deaf to me at all
Lest, if Thou silent be to me,
I like those in the pit shall be.
> *Refrain*
> O save Thy people, Lord, and bless
> Thy Church, Thine own inheritance;
> And be our Shepherd also, Lord,
> And carry us forever more.

O hear my supplications, Lord,
And let my cries to Thee be heard;
When I my hands lift up to Thee,
And cry for help to rescue me.
> *Refrain*

Lord, drag me not away with them
Who wickedly Thy Law condemn.
Because Thy works they do not heed
Thou shalt destroy them with all speed.
> *Refrain*

Blessed be the Lord! For He has heard
My plaintive cry and humble word.
He is my strength, He is my shield,
And I am helped when to Him I yield.
> *Refrain*

We trust in Thee and with one voice
Now thank and praise Thee and rejoice!
Thou art our strength; Lord Jesus be
Our sure Defense for eternity!
> *Refrain*

# Psalm 60

*vv. 1-4: Thy people confess their sad and sorry state.*

O God, Thou has cast us off, Thou hast scattered us, Thou has been displeased; O turn Thyself to us again. Thou hast made the earth to tremble; Thou hast broken it: Heal the breaches thereof; for it shaketh. Thou hast shewed Thy people hard things: Thou hast made us to drink the wine of astonishment. Thou hast given a banner to them that fear Thee, that may be displayed because of the truth.

*vv. 5-8: Reminded of God's promise to inherit the nations, they cry to Him for deliverance.*

That Thy beloved may be delivered; save with Thy right hand, and hear me. God hath spoken in His holiness; I will rejoice, I will divide Shechem, and mete out the valley of Succoth. Gilead is mine, and Manasseh is mine; Ephraim also is the strength of mine head; Judah is my lawgiver; Moab is my washpot, over Edom will I cast out my shoe: Philistia, triumph thou because of Me.

*vv.9-12: The people look to God for revival and for victory over their enemies.*

Who will bring me into the strong city? Who will lead me into Edom? Wilt not Thou, O God, which hadst cast us off? And Thou, O God, which didst not go out with our armies? Give us help from trouble: For vain is the help of man. Through God we shall do valiantly: For He it is that shall tread down our enemies.

## Psalm 60 (vv. 1-5, 10-12)
### Tune: St. Anne ('Our God, Our Help in Ages Past')

O God, You have rejected us, Your anger we have known;
Your wrath has broken out on us; restore us as Your own!

The earth You have in anger split; it quakes with bitter groans.
Repair its breaches, lest it fall; restore us as Your own!

Your people stagger as when drunk; through hardship we have
grown.
Your truth unfurled declares Your love; restore us as Your own!

O may Your loved ones rescued be, who cry to you alone.
Save with Your right hand, answer us; restore us as Your own!

Have not You, Lord, rejected us? And shall we fight alone?
Return with us to battle, Lord; restore us as Your own!

Against the foe of all our souls in mighty tumult thrown,
Through You we shall do valiantly; restore us as Your own!

For Christ has tread the devil down; He rules upon His throne!
He ev'ry enemy subdues; restore us as Your own!

# Psalm 79

*vv. 1-4: The people bemoan the sad state of their nation.*

O God, the heathen are come into Thine inheritance; Thy holy temple have they defiled; they have laid Jerusalem on heaps. The dead bodies of Thy servants have they given to be meat unto the fowls of the heaven, the flesh of Thy saints unto the beasts of the earth. Their blood have they shed like water round about Jerusalem; and there was none to bury them. We are become a reproach to our neighbours, a scorn and derision to them that are round about us.

*vv. 5-7: They plead with God to destroy their foes.*

How long, Lord? Wilt Thou be angry forever? Shall Thy jealousy burn like fire? Pour out Thy wrath upon the heathen that have not known Thee, and upon the kingdoms that have not called upon Thy name. For they have devoured Jacob, and laid waste his dwelling place.

*v. 8: The people confess their sin to God.*

O remember not against us former iniquities: Let Thy tender mercies speedily prevent us; for we are brought very low.

*vv. 9-12: They seek His help and deliverance.*

Help us, O God of our salvation, for the glory of Thy name: And deliver us, and purge away our sins, for Thy name's sake. Wherefore should the heathen say, Where is their God? Let Him be known among the heathen in our sight by the revenging of the blood of Thy servants which is shed. Let the sighing of the prisoner come before Thee; according to the greatness of Thy power preserve Thou those that are appointed to die; and render unto our neighbours sevenfold into their bosom their reproach, wherewith they have reproached Thee, O Lord.

*v. 13: The people confess their trust in the Lord alone.*

So we Thy people and sheep of Thy pasture will give Thee thanks forever: We will shew forth Thy praise to all generations.

## Psalm 79 (vv. 1, 4, 5, 8, 9, 13)
### Tune: Tryggare Kan Ingen Vara L. M.
### ('Children of the Heavenly Father')

O God, the nations sinful have defiled Your holy temple;
They have ruined Your holy city, on Your people shown no pity.


We are scoffed and oft derided, by our neighbors cruelly chided.
Will Your anger last forever? Will Your wrath be quenched never?


Lord, O mind not the transgressions of the former generations;
Let Your love be quick to woo us, and Your mercy hasten to us.


Help us, God of our salvation, us Your chosen generation;
Save us, Lord; Lord, please forgive us; for Your glory, grant
deliv'rance.


We the people of Your pasture will give thanks to You forever;
We will publish all your praises to the coming generation.

# Psalm 85

*vv. 1-3: The people recall the renewing mercy of God to previous generations.*

Lord, Thou hast been favourable unto Thy land: Thou hast brought back the captivity of Jacob. Thou hast forgiven the iniquity of Thy people, Thou hast covered all their sin. Thou hast taken away all Thy wrath: Thou hast turned Thyself from the fierceness of Thine anger.

*vv. 4-7: On that basis, they cry out to God to deliver and renew them.*

Turn us, O God of our salvation, and cause Thine anger toward us to cease. Wilt Thou be angry with us forever? Wilt Thou draw out Thine anger to all generations? Wilt Thou not revive us again: That Thy people may rejoice in Thee? Shew us Thy mercy, O Lord, and grant us Thy salvation.

*vv. 8-11: The people express their confidence that God will answer their prayer.*

I will hear what God the Lord will speak: For He will speak peace unto His people and to His saints: But let them not turn again to folly. Surely His salvation is nigh them that fear Him; that glory may dwell in our land. Mercy and truth are met together; righteousness and peace have kissed each other. Truth shall spring out of the earth; and righteousness shall look down from heaven.

*vv. 12, 13: They express their hope and trust in the Lord's renewing grace.*

Yea, the Lord shall give that which is good; and our land shall yield her increase. Righteousness shall go before Him; and shall set us in the way of His steps.

## Psalm 85

Tune: Meirionydd ('O Savior, Precious Savior')


O Lord, You showed Your favor to Israel of old;
From bondage You did save her, for so the prophets told.
Their sins were then forgiven, You covered all their stains;
Your wrath from them was driven, and peace restored again.


Restore us, God our Savior! And turn Your wrath away!
Renew us to Your favor; the rod of chast'ning stay.
O Lord, will You revive us? Let us rejoice in You.
Bestow Your lovingkindness; our faith and church renew.


O let us heed Your Word, Lord, as peace to us You speak;
And keep us in Your Word, Lord, nor let us folly seek.
Your grace is near to all who in fear and rev'rence bow,
And who devote themselves to your glory here and now.


Now truth and lovingkindness are joined in Christ our King!
And righteousness and peace kiss in Him Whose praise we sing!
The Lord will grant His goodness that we may faithful be;
His righteousness shall lead us; His pathway we shall see.

# Annotated Bibliography

## John H. Armstrong

It is helpful for all who pray for revival and have a keen interest in the subject to read and think more widely about it. This bibliography is not exhaustive nor is it one that includes only those titles that I personally agree with on every point. I have listed these titles because of their general value for those who wish to pursue the subject further. I have also chosen books that appear to be either still in print or fairly accessible. The serious student may wish to search for them.

Alexander, Archibald. *The Log College*. Edinburgh, Scotland: Banner of Truth, 1968 reprint of 1851 edition. The 'log college' was the name contemptuously given to the ministerial college that was the forerunner of Princeton Seminary. Includes biographical sketches of William Tennent and students greatly used in revival ministry during the First Great Awakening.

Anderson, Neil T. and Elmer L. Towns. *Rivers of Revival*. Ventura, California: Regal, 1997. One of the most recent products of the theology of revivalism, this book is both interesting and distressing. If you want to compare two modern popularly written books on revival with an entirely opposite perspective compare this title with *True Revival: What Happens When God's Spirit Moves?*

Armstrong, John H. *True Revival: What Happens When God's Spirit Moves?* Eugene, Oregon: Harvest House, 2001. Seeks to answer questions such as: How do true revivals take place? What are the unique marks of true revival? How do we prepare our own hearts for such a move of God's Spirit? J. I Packer says, '[*True Revival*] contains one of the most perceptive discussions of revival you will find anywhere.'

Armstrong, John H., ed. *The Coming Evangelical Crisis: Current Challenges to the Authority of Scripture and the Gospel.* Chicago: Moody Press, 1996. Includes essays by a number of evangelical leaders who are all concerned that evangelicalism now faces a 'crisis.' This crisis has come because of the ravaging effects of revivalism.

Armstrong, John H., ed. *Crisis in the Evangelical Church: Worship Sacraments and Piety.* Wheaton, Illinois: Crossway, 1998. This is a companion volume to the one listed above and addresses how the 'crisis' can be seen in the doctrine and life of the church. Unless we recover a sound view of the church we will compound revivalistic solutions.

Armstrong, John H. *Five Great Evangelists: Preachers of Real Revival.* Fearn, Ross-shire, Scotland: Christian Focus Publications, 1997. A biographical introduction to five of the most wonderfully used evangelists in the history of Christianity. Each was a preacher who knew the presence and blessing of real revival.

Azurdia, Arturo G., III. *Spirit Empowered Preaching: Involving the Holy Spirit in Your Ministry.* Fearn, Ross-shire,

Scotland: Christian Focus Publications, 1998. The most important book available on preaching and the power of God's Spirit in awakening hearers to grace. Every minister ought to read it and pray that God's empowerment will rest upon their ministry.

Blackaby, Henry T. and Claude V. King. *Experiencing God: Knowing and Doing the Will of God*. Nashville: Baptist Sunday School Board, 1992. A very popular small group guide that is useful but flawed by its theology.

Blackaby, Henry T. *Fresh Encounter*. Nashville: Broadman & Holman Publishers, 1996. A study of revival principles that is once again flawed by revivalistic theology.

Bright, Bill. *The Coming Revival: America's Call to Fast, Pray, and 'Seek God's Face.'* Orlando, Florida: NewLife Publications, 1995. This book is one of the leading examples of revivalism and its bizarre claims regarding modern revival.

Bryant, David. *The Hope At Hand: National and World Revival for the Twenty-First Century*. Grand Rapids: Baker, 1995. Bryant, best known for his leadership of the 'Concerts of Prayer' movement is an engaging proponent of revival prayer. The weakness is that he is not sufficiently careful theologically to escape several of the pitfalls of revivalism.

Bryant, David. *Stand in the Gap: How to Prepare for the Coming World Revival*. Ventura, California: Regal Books, 1997. The book's cover proclaims the view that 'an awesome move of God is unfolding across our nation and across the planet . . .' Useful but still needs to be balanced by older, theologically careful, books.

Buchanan, James. *The Office and Work of the Holy Spirit.* Edinburgh, Scotland: Banner of Truth, 1966 reprint of 1843 edition. Includes a clear and rich section on revival rarely found today.

Duewel, Wesley. *Revival Fire.* Grand Rapids: Zondervan, 1995. Though I do not share Duewel's Wesleyan theology, this is an excellent book in many ways.

Edwards, Brian H. *Revival! A People Saturated With God.* Darlington, County Durham, England: Evangelical Press, 1990. This is one of the four or five best general titles on the subject that the average reader should procure. Filled with accounts and stories as well as wise pastoral counsel.

Ellsworth, Roger. *Come Down, Lord!* Edinburgh, Scotland: Banner of Truth, 1988. A very good little book (56 pages) which introduces the subject very biblically.

Evans, Eifion. *Fire in the Thatch: The True Nature of Religious Revival.* Bryntirion, Bridgend, Wales: Evangelical Press of Wales, 1996. Evans is one of the most helpful historians of revival writing today. His special interest is his own country of Wales, 'the land of awakenings.'

Fawcett, Arthur. *The Cambuslang Revival: The Scottish Evangelical Revival of the Eighteenth Century.* Edinburgh, Scotland: Banner of Truth, 1971. An exciting story well told.

Finney, Charles G. *Finney's Systematic Theology*. Minneapolis: Bethany House Publishers, 1994 reprint of 1878 edition. This definitive edition of Finney will demonstrate to the discerning and careful reader just how far he drifted from any semblance of orthodoxy.

Finney, Charles G. *The Memoirs of Charles G. Finney: An Annotated Critical Edition* (Garth M. Rosell & Richard A. G. Dupuis, editors). Grand Rapids: Zondervan, 1989. This full edition is extremely important for serious scholars. It shows Finney as he really was, not as public relations people have sought to make him.

Finney, Charles G. *Revivals of Religion*. Grand Rapids: Fleming H. Revell, n.d. The famous manual that promotes the steps one should take to *guarantee* revival.

Fish, Henry C. *Handbook of Revivals*. Harrisonburg, Virginia: Gano Books, 1988 reprint of 1874 edition. The title should not keep you from this useful and immensely practical book.

Goen, C. G., ed. *The Works of Jonathan Edwards*, Volume 4: 'The Great Awakening.' New Haven, Connecticut: Yale University Press, 1972. This is the academic and richly annotated edition of the several important works of Edwards on revival. For less money and without annotations get the Banner of Truth editions.

Hanegraaff, Hank. *Counterfeit Revival: Looking for God in All the Wrong Places*. Dallas: Word, 1997. An expose of the various 'counterfeit' movements of revival that have swept North America in the last ten years or so. Hanegraaff will show you that these movements have gone far beyond older Pentecostalism and are positively dangerous. Particularly critical of both the 'Toronto Blessing' and the 'Brownsville Revival.'

Hardman, Keith J. *Seasons of Refreshing: Evangelism and Revivals in America.* Grand Rapids: Baker, 1994. Hardman, who wrote the best biography available on Charles G. Finney, is a good historian. He traces the development of mass evangelism in America in this book.

Hayden, Eric. *Praying for Revival.* Fearn, Ross-shire, Scotland: Christian Focus Publications, 2001. The author clearly understands revival in the right sense and thereby offers wise and important counsel on prayer and its relationship to true revival. A choice book.

Hulse, Erroll. *Give Him No Rest: A Call to Prayer for Revival.* Darlington, County Durham, England: Evangelical Press, 1991. The best in-print book available on how prayer relates to revival and why we ought to 'give Him no rest' in our pleas for the fulfillment of His commission and the world encompassing promises of Gospel success.

Kaiser, Walter C. Jr. *Revive Us Again: Biblical Insights for Encouraging Spiritual Renewal.* Fearn, Ross-shire, Scotland: Christian Focus Publications, 2001. A readable, yet scholarly, overview of the spiritual principles inherent in great awakenings found in the Bible. Lessons can and should be learned from the great revivals recorded in the Scripture. Kaiser is an excellent guide.

Lloyd-Jones, D. Martyn. *Revival*. Wheaton, Illinois: Crossway, 1987. Dr. J. I. Packer calls this the most 'powerful [and] profound treatment of revival' seen in our age. It is a 'must' read for anyone serious about this subject.

Lloyd-Jones, D. Martyn. *The Puritans: Their Origins and Successors*. Edinburgh, Scotland: Banner of Truth, 1987. Includes a number of lectures Lloyd-Jones gave at the Puritan and Westminster Conferences in London between 1959 and 1978. Includes his marvelous lectures: 'Revival: An Historical and Theological Survey', 'Howell Harris and Revival', and 'Jonathan Edwards and the Crucial Importance of Revival.' This is church history and practical theology at its very best!

McDow, Malcolm, and Alvin L. Reid. *Firefall: How God Has Shaped History Through Revivals*. Nashville: Broadman & Holman Publishers, 1997. A very helpful historical overview though the theological arguments are not carefully thought out and the conclusions are affected.

Murray, Iain H. *Revival & Revivalism: The Making and Marring of American Evangelicalism 1750-1858*. Edinburgh, Scotland: Banner of Truth, 1994. If you read only one *serious* book on the history of revival and revivalism make it this one. This is the most interesting and important book available on the subject of how and why American revivalism arose.

Murray, Iain H. *The Puritan Hope: Revival and the Interpretation of Prophecy*. Edinburgh, Scotland: Banner of Truth, 1971. Even if you do not share all the views outlined in this volume you will not be able to easily put this exciting book down. It wonderfully fueled my own hope for God to revive us.

Murray, Iain H. *Jonathan Edwards: A New Biography*. Edinburgh, Scotland: Banner of Truth, 1987. The best modern biography of Jonathan Edwards. A must for understanding the man and the ministry behind the theologian of revival. Modern promoters of Edwards' idea of 'Concerts of Prayer' should read Murray and grasp the profound God-centeredness of Edwards.

Olford, Stephen F. *Heart-Cry for Revival: Expository Sermons on Revival*. Grand Rapids: Fleming H. Revell, 1962. A good wake up call to prayer and concern for revival.

Orr, J. Edwin. *The Event of the Century: The 1857-1858 Awakening*. Wheaton, Illinois: International Awakening Press, 1989. A thorough and useful study by a respected historian of revival.

Ortlund, Raymond C., Jr. *When God Comes to Church: A Biblical Model for Revival Today*. Grand Rapids: Baker, 2000. Perhaps the best biblical exposition of the subject of revival currently available, especially as it is rooted in the Old Testament text. Solid, careful, accurate, and most practical.

Packer, J. I. *A Quest for Godliness: The Puritan Vision of the Christian Life*. Wheaton, Illinois: Crossway, 1990. This collection of essays on the Puritans includes several important chapters on revival that should not be missed. It is a vivid, warm and immensely useful book.

Phillips, Thomas. *The Welsh Revival: Its Origin & Development*. Edinburgh, Scotland: Banner of Truth, 1989 reprint of 1860 edition. The first comprehensive account of this very remarkable revival.

Porter, Ebenezer. *Letters on Revival*. Brooklyn, New York: Linde Publications, 1992. This reprint of 1832 volume is rich. Porter, a Congregational minister, strongly opposed the rise of Finneyism. His counsel might help us get out of some of the problems created in the 1830s.

Prime, Samuel. *The Power of Prayer: The New York Revival of 1858*. Edinburgh, Scotland: Banner of Truth, 1991 reprint of 1859 edition. A very stimulating first-hand account.

Reid, William. *Authentic Records of Revival*. Richard Owen Roberts Publishers, 1980 reprint of 1860 edition. A good account of the awakening that happened in 1860.

Roberts, Richard Owen. *Revival!* Wheaton, Illinois: Richard Owen Roberts Publishers, 1982. A most important book. The author has considered revival for nearly fifty years. The section on hindrances is worth the book.

Roberts, Richard Owen, ed. *Salvation in Full Color: Twenty Sermons by Great Awakening Preachers*. Wheaton, Illinois:

International Awakening Press, 1994. An excellent set of sermons showing the kind of preaching that has been visited with the power of true revival.

Roberts, Richard Owen, ed. *Sanctify the Congregation: A Call to the Solemn Assembly and to Corporate Repentance*. Wheaton, Illinois: International Awakening Press, 1994. Contains fifteen doctrinal sermons that were useful in calling the church to repentance and the need for revival in days past.

Smeaton, George. *The Doctrine of the Holy Spirit*. Edinburgh, Scotland: Banner of Truth, 1974 reprint of 1889 edition. Smeaton, a Presbyterian theologian, has given us a sound pneumatology that includes the older view of revival.

Sprague, William B. *Lectures on Revivals*. Edinburgh, Scotland: Banner of Truth, 1959 reprint of 1832 edition. This is a classic. Lloyd-Jones highly regarded this reprinted work. Sprague was a prominent historian and church leader during the Second Great Awakening.

Thomas, I. D. E. *God's Harvest: The Nature of True Revival*. Bryntirion, Bridgend, Wales: Evangelical Press of Wales, 1997. Only 62 pages, this recent reprint is clear, beneficial and warm.

Thornbury, John F. *God Sent Revival: The Story of Asahel Nettleton and the Second Great Awakening*. Darlington, County Durham, England, 1977. If you wish to see the life of the greatest itinerant evangelist of the old school approach, read this biography. It is a marvelous and thrilling book.

Tracy, Joseph. *The Great Awakening: A History of the Revival of Religion in the Time of Edwards and Whitefield*. Edinburgh, Scotland: Banner of Truth, 1976 reprint of 1842 edition. Often criticized for coining the phrase 'The Great Awakening' this is a profitable book, if for no other reason than that it shows something of the marvelous deeds of the Lord during this time period.

Tyler, Bennet. *New England Revivals*. Wheaton, Illinois: Richard Owen Roberts Publishers, 1980. These accounts appeared in the Connecticut Evangelical Magazine from 1797 until 1802. This is some of the most inspiring record of revival I have ever personally read. I have read these accounts to church gatherings in order to encourage prayer groups for revival.

Wells, David F. *No Place for Truth, Or Whatever Happened to Evangelical Theology?* Grand Rapids: Eerdmans, 1993. Wells presents the most penetrating analysis available of the state of modern evangelicalism. A 'must' book for serious leaders, especially in North America.

Wright, Eric H. *Strange Fire? Assessing the Vineyard Movement and the Toronto Blessing*. Darlington, County Durham, England: Evangelical Press, 1996. Many critiques on this movement have been written, both pro and con. This is the best *critical* approach I have read. Wright has a sound view of revival and applies it carefully to this much-studied movement.

# Notes

## Introduction

[1] Solomon Stoddard, 'On the Occasion of an Unusual Outpouring of the Spirit of God,' in Keith J. Hardman, ed., *Issues in American Christianity* (Grand Rapids: Baker Books, 1993), p. 47.

[2] Iain H. Murray, *Revival and Revivalism* (Edinburgh: Banner of Truth, 1994), p. 24.

[3] Thomas Cahill, *How the Irish Saved Civilization* (New York: Doubleday, 1995).

[4] Although some would also consider the period of the 1960s to possess many of the historic marks of revival. See, for example, Robert S. Wellwood, *The Sixties Spiritual Awakening* (New Brunswick: Rutgers University Press, 1994).

[5] Cf. Edith L. Blumhofer and Randall Balmer, eds., *Modern Christian Revivals* (Urbana: University of Illinois Press, 1993) and Michael J. Crawford, *Seasons of Grace* (Oxford: Oxford University Press, 1991).

[6] Jonathan Edwards, 'The Distinguishing Marks of a Work of the Spirit of God,' in *Jonathan Edwards on Revival* (Edinburgh: Banner of Truth, 1995), p. 130, italics in the original.

[7] *Ibid.*, p. 131.

[8] Cf. David Bryant, *The Hope at Hand* (Grand Rapids: Baker Books, 1995).

[9] Alexander Cumming, in Ministers of the Church of Scotland, *Lectures on the Revival of Religion* (Wheaton: Richard Owen Roberts, Publishers, 1980 [1840]), p. 141.

## 1. Waiting on the Lord

[1] Cumming, in Ministers of the Church of Scotland, p. 135.

[2] Murray, p. 131.

[3] See on, chapter 4.

[4] Jonathan Edwards, 'An Humble Attempt to Promote Explicit Agreement and Visible Union of God's People in Extraordinary Prayer for the Revival of Religion and the Advancement of Christ's Kingdom on Earth,' in Edward Hickman, ed., *The Works of Jonathan Edwards*, Vol. 2 (Edinburgh: Banner of Truth, 1995), p. 281.

[5] J. Edwin Orr, 'Power in United Prayer,' in *Prayer: Its Deeper Dimensions: A Christian Life Symposium* (Grand Rapids: Zondervan, 1963), pp. 20-26.

[6] Orr, p. 20.

[7] William Burns, in Ministers of the Church of Scotland, p. 334.

## 2. Setting Your House in Order

[1] John Bonar, in *Ministers of the Church of Scotland*, p. 9.

[2] Murray, p. 129.

[3] See on, chapter 3.

## 3. A Spirit of Sacrifice

[1] W. M. H. in Ministers of the Church of Scotland, p. xviii.

[2] 1 Pet. 4:3, 4; 1 Cor. 1:18; cf. also the charges that arose in the second century in northern Asia Minor, where Christians were accused of incest and cannibalism.

[3] It has sometimes been argued that the early Christians, according to Acts 4:34, practiced a form of communism,

renouncing all private property for the greater good of the whole community. However, the form of the verb, *hyperchon*, 'would give up' (NASB), being in the imperfect, suggests a habitual practice as need arose, not a once-for-all depositing of possessions into the hands of community leaders.

## 4. A Vision for Revival

[1] Cf. various works by Thomas Sowell, Franz Schurmann, Leighton Ford, and others.

## Afterword: Leading the Way

[1] Murray, pp. 127, 26.

[2] Murray, p. 129.

[3] William Burns, in Ministers of the Church of Scotland, p. 336.

[4] John Calvin, Letter to the Church of Geneva, 1 October 1538, in Henry Beveridge and Jules Bonnet, eds., *Selected Works of John Calvin: Tracts and Letters*, Vol. IV, tr. by David Constable (Grand Rapids: Baker Book House, 1983), p. 88.

## Reformation & Revival Ministries

Reformation & Revival Ministries, in a partnership with Christian Focus Publications, began an imprint line of books in the year 2000 for the purpose of providing resources for the reformation of the Christian church through the life and work of Christian leaders. Our goal is to publish and distribute new works of pastoral and theological substance aimed at reforming the leadership, life and vision of the church around the world.

Reformation & Revival Ministries was incorporated in 1991, through the labors of John H. Armstrong, who had been a pastor for the previous twenty-one years, for the purpose of serving the church as an educational and evangelistic resource. The desire from the beginning has been to encourage doctrinal and ethical reformation joined with informed prayer for spiritual awakening. The foundational convictions of the ministry can be summarized in the great truths of the sixteenth century Protestant Reformation and the evangelical revivals of the eighteenth and nineteenth centuries.

To accomplish this vision the ministry publishes a quarterly journal (since 1992), *Reformation & Revival Journal*, designed for pastors and serious readers of theology and church renewal. A more popular magazine, *Viewpoint*, is published six times per year. The ministry also has an extensive array of books and tapes.

Dr. Armstrong speaks in conferences, local churches and various ministerial groups across the United States and abroad. The ministry has a no debt policy and is financed only by the gifts of interested people. The policy from the beginning has been to never ask for funds through solicitation, believing that God provides as he will, where he will, and when he will. An office and support staff operate the ministry in suburban Chicago.

Further information on the ministry and the above resources can be found in the following ways:

Reformation & Revival Ministries
P. O. Box 88216
Carol Stream, Illinois 60188
(630) 980-1810
(630) 980-1820, Fax

E-mail: RRMinistry@aol.com    Web: www.randr.org

T. M. Moore is Pastor of Teaching Ministries at Cedar Springs Presbyterian Church in Knoxville, Tennessee. In addition, he serves as Associate for Ministry Advancement with Reformation and Revival Ministries. His most recent books are *Celtic Flame: The Burden of Patrick* and *Ecclesiastes*. He and his wife, Susie, have four children and nine grandchildren.

This book is dedicated to the memory of
Dr. J. Edwin Orr,
who first opened my mind to understand the nature of
revival and the possibilities for knowing such an
outpouring of God's grace in our day.